A most needed book. I often meet with parents who are seeking direction about how to handle adult children who have spurned the Christian beliefs, values, and standards of their parents. This book will be of immense help. Thanks, Jim and Elyse, for giving parents a biblically based book with solid guidelines for knowing the most God-honoring and helpful way to navigate this valley. May God use this volume to strengthen parents in this situation and help them point the way back to him all the clearer.

—**Wayne A. Mack**, Professor of Biblical Counseling, Grace School of Ministry in Pretoria and Capetown, South Africa

Wise, compassionate, much-needed counsel for parents of adult (or nearly adult) children. Jim and Elyse clearly present the responsibilities of lifelong biblical parenting solidly within the context of God's absolute sovereignty. I'm not aware of another book like it on the market today and highly recommend it to all who truly desire to rightly influence their children all the days of their lives.

—**Carol J. Ruvolo**, Conference Speaker, Author of Bible Studies including *No Other Gospel* and *Before the Throne of God*

Jim Newheiser and Elyse Fitzpatrick have given the church a Christ-centered, biblically and practically wise book, seasoned with rich experience as counselors and parents. Although books on parenthood seem to never end, here is a unique contribution that deals with an issue that is by and large ignored: parenthood and adult children. They cover the multifaceted issues with skill and grace. As a pastor who counsels and a parent of adult children, I am very thankful for this book. I will be using it and distributing it in our church.

—**Brian Borgman**, Pastor, Grace Community Church, Minden, NV

The question of how parents should relate to their adult children, who too often have an entitlement mindset while at the same time refusing to take the hard and sacrificial steps to become independently functioning adults, has become a minefield of potential conflict. So how do you cut the apron strings? What does love demand? What does God expect? And how can parents sort through the turmoil of knowing when, where, how much, and how long to help? The authors wisely and humbly guide us through some of the biggest struggles, basing their answers on biblical principles as well as personal experience gained from their own lives and the hours they've spent counseling others. This book doesn't give pat, easy answers, but it does offer hope and practical steps for how to please God that are buoyed with grace and humility. As a parent of five children who are now making their own transition into adulthood, I was convicted, encouraged, and strengthened to do better. I'll be turning to this book again and again and passing it on to others who are looking for godly counsel as they walk through what can be a confusing season of figuring out how to relate to young adults who are no longer children, but will always be your child.

—**Brad Bigney**, Senior Pastor, Grace Fellowship Church, Florence, KY

This is a wonderful book written for parents who are hurting and want solid biblical answers that speak to the heart. This is not a book on mere parental techniques or behavioral changes. It is a book that takes parents to the foot of the cross and causes them to take an honest look at their own hearts and their parenting. Furthermore, it is not a book on parenting theories; it is a book born from years of the real-life parenting and counseling experiences of both of the authors. If you are a struggling parent, this book will bring you refreshing hope in handling your role from a biblical perspective.

—**John D. Street**, Chair, Master of Arts in Biblical Counseling Graduate Program, The Master's College and Seminary

I never speak on the topic of raising children without facing the inevitable questions about how to respond to adult children who are struggling with the transition between childhood and adulthood. *You Never Stop Being a Parent* answers the most frequently asked questions with biblical clarity, wisdom, and insight. This book will help parents to think with clarity about the many issues raised by interacting with adult children. The answers it gives are not only clear and practical, but richly gospel-centered and filled with hope. This is a book I will buy in bulk and recommend to many.

—**Tedd Tripp**, Pastor, Conference Speaker, Author of *Shepherding a Child's Heart*

Jim Newheiser and Elyse Fitzpatrick have given the body of Christ an excellent treasure in *You Never Stop Being a Parent*. There is no other Christian book quite like it. With a solid biblical background guiding the principles they share, with practical wisdom from many years of their own in-home and now out-of-home parenting, and with direct but sensitive admonishment for those parents who are struggling to build lasting, godly relationships with their adult children, these two parent counselors have provided us with a great deal of valuable assistance. So as parents of adult children, whether you are frustrated or fulfilled, may this helpful volume bring you much encouragement.

—**Lance Quinn**, Pastor-Teacher, The Bible Church of Little Rock

Elyse Fitzpatrick and Jim Newheiser have written a very practical book based on biblical principles to help parents of adult children. The style is engaging and the advice very wise. I wish that I had had this book years ago, before our oldest child got married!

—**Martha Peace**, Biblical Counselor, Author of
*The Excellent Wife* and *Damsels in Distress*

Perfect timing. Just as the questions from parents with adult children start streaming in, we have solid, biblical material to put in their hands. And the book is packed. No sooner did I think, "But what about . . ." before the next illustration set me off on a wise course. Thank you.

—**Ed Welch**, Director of Counseling, Christian
Counseling and Educational Foundation

Sometimes these later years can be some of the most challenging for parents, but in this book you will find lots of direction, compassion, and hope. The reader will quickly catch that the authors are fellow sinners and fellow sufferers who speak to us as brother and sister in the Lord. From this humble perspective, several "hot" issues (courtship, parental authority, in-laws, grandparents, etc.) are dealt with biblically, using lots of real-life stories and practical applications to help the reader see how the principles are lived out in real life. The authors stress the importance of relationships giving priority to the parent's own heart and responses and to the marriage bond. As they flesh out what it means to be loving, faithful, and courageous and to trust God with our children, they continually point us to the person of Christ and all the resources we have as Christians—the Spirit, the Word, the church, and so on. After all this, the appendices at the end of the book again offer important practical helps such as tools for resolving conflicts and sample contracts between parents and young adults. This is one book that every parent needs to have and read!

—**Stuart W. Scott**, *Executive Director,*
*National Center of Biblical Counseling*

# You Never Stop Being a Parent

# You Never Stop Being a Parent

## Thriving in Relationship with Your Adult Children

Jim Newheiser and Elyse Fitzpatrick

P U B L I S H I N G

P.O. BOX 817 • PHILLIPSBURG • NEW JERSEY 08865-0817

Unless otherwise indicated, Scripture quotations are from *ESV Bible* ® (*The Holy Bible, English Standard Version* ®). Copyright © 2001 by Crossway Bibles, a publishing ministry of Good News Publishers. Used by permission. All rights reserved.

Scripture quotations marked (NASB) are from the NEW AMERICAN STAN-DARD BIBLE®. Copyright © 1960, 1962, 1963, 1968, 1971, 1972, 1973, 1975, 1977, 1995 by The Lockman Foundation. Used by permission.

Printed in the United States of America

**Library of Congress Cataloging-in-Publication Data**

Newheiser, Jim.
  You never stop being a parent : thriving in relationship with your adult children / Jim Newheiser and Elyse Fitzpatrick.
      p. cm.
  Includes bibliographical references (p.      ).
  ISBN 978-1-59638-174-2 (pbk.)
  1. Parenting–Religious aspects–Christianity. 2. Parent and adult child–Religious aspects–Christianity. 3. Adult children–Family relationships. 4. Intergenerational relations–Religious aspects–Christianity. I. Fitzpatrick, Elyse, 1950- II. Title.
  BV4529.N49 2010
  248.8'450844–dc22
                                                                         2010010197

To
Jim and Caroline,
loving parents and faithful servants

—E.F.


In memory of my father and my grandfather,
both of whom exemplified many of the principles in this
book,
and with thanks to the parents and adult kids
who opened their hearts to us,
allowing us to use their stories to help others

—J.N.

# Contents

# CONTENTS

# Introduction

SEVERAL YEARS AGO, I concluded a sermon on child training by saying that our parenting responsibilities finally end when our children become adults. After the service, one of our older friends, Elmer, put his arm around me, smiled, and said, "Jim, you never stop being a parent." I had no idea then how true his words would be in my life.

At the time, our kids were all still at home, but Elmer's comment made me think. I observed how he and his wife, Evelyn, were still very involved in the lives of their children, some of whom were close to my age. For instance, when one of their sons was injured, Elmer traveled across the country to be at his side and help keep his business afloat until he recovered. Another son and his wife are missionaries in Mexico,

Although this book is a collaboration between Jim Newheiser and Elyse Fitzpatrick, unless otherwise specified, all of the first-person statements are Jim's. Scattered frequently throughout the book, you'll also find personal testimonies or advice from parents just like you. These statements were culled from Jim's counseling experiences and from surveys of families whose stories probably intersect with yours in many ways. Permission to use these statements was given and all identifying names and situations were changed.

and they often visited them and shared in their ministry. In addition to making these frequent out-of-town trips, Evelyn was also involved in homeschooling a granddaughter who lived in the area. Elmer's life proved his point. He never stopped being a parent.

My understanding of our ongoing responsibilities as parents grew when I read a story in our local newspaper about a woman who was celebrating her 105th birthday. Discussing her closeness to her children, the article quoted her as saying, "Well, they're not kids anymore, but they are to me." Her children were seventy-four and seventy-five years old, and even though they had been adults for over half a century, they were still her "kids." And, as I began to learn, if you have children of your own, you'll never stop calling them your "kids" either.

Over the past several years, my wife and I have watched our three sons enter into adulthood. We're thankful that we have good relationships with each of them. We have learned a lot as we watched our boys turn into men, but the truth is that this transition involved a steep learning curve for us. While we were traversing these sometimes stormy days, I often felt like we were in uncharted waters. I tried to find biblical resources to help us navigate these rocky shoals, but nothing was available. Of course, there were plenty of solid Christian books about parenting young children. In recent years, there have even been some very useful additions about parenting adolescents and dealing with teenage rebellion. But there wasn't anything that addressed the unique challenges Caroline and I were facing—challenges that confronted both us as parents and our sons as adult children.

The conflicts and difficulties between parents and their adult kids aren't merely issues among Christians, either. *Time* magazine had a cover story about the social phenomenon of "twixters," a term referring to adults who are still living at home[1] and who remain in-between adulthood and childhood. In many ways, they're more like overgrown kids when it comes to managing mature responsibilities.[2] In the movie *Failure to Launch*, Matthew McConaughey portrays a typical twixter, a thirty-something slacker who has finally driven his parents to desperation. Determined to be free from this albatross, they hire an expert to engineer circumstances that, they hope, will launch their son out of their home. While things don't work out exactly as they planned, their son does finally move out, and the film ends with the parents gladly singing, "Hit the Road Jack."

That this twixter phenomenon is becoming part of our day-to-day lives was made plain to me a few months ago while walking through the Phoenix airport. I saw a young man sporting a t-shirt that boldly declared, "I still live with my parents." I knew that he was making an attempt at humor, but I wondered why he would wear a shirt like that.

The Christian community is facing unique challenges of its own regarding this problem, as many young adults are deciding to leave the faith after being raised in Christian homes. Barna research reports that six out of ten 20-somethings who were involved in church during their teen years have dropped out of actively participating in Christian activities.[3] In recent years, as the first generation of homeschooled kids are graduating and entering adulthood, many have failed to meet the high expectations of their parents. These are not children who fail to leave home. These are children who fail to embrace the faith of their home. Homeschool leader Reb Bradley writes,

> In the last couple of years, I have heard from multitudes of troubled homeschool parents around the country, a good many of whom were leaders. These parents have graduated their first batch of kids, only to discover that their children didn't turn out the way they thought they would. Many of

these children were model homeschoolers while growing up, but sometime after their eighteenth birthday they began to reveal that they didn't hold to their parents' values. Some of these young people grew up and left home in defiance of their parents. Others got married against their parents' wishes, and still others got involved with drugs, alcohol, and immorality. I have even heard of several exemplary young men who no longer believe in God. My own adult children have gone through struggles I never guessed they would have faced. Most of these parents remain stunned by their children's choices, because they were fully confident their approach to parenting was going to prevent any such rebellion.[4]

Well-intentioned parents, who have devoted two decades of their lives trying to shape their children, are having a hard time letting go of their adult kids, especially when they make choices of which they do not approve. What authority do parents have over their grown kids? What should parents do if their children make choices with which they disagree? One parent we interviewed writes, "Somehow, we thought that when the children reached eighteen, our parenting would be pretty much over. On the contrary, we discovered that our most challenging years as parents were in the vicinity of ages eighteen to twenty-three. . . . When the children were small, parenting was simple—not easy, but simple." Another parent wrote, "I would have never imagined it would be this hard."

In addition to relating with our own adult sons, I also serve as a biblical counselor with the Institute for Biblical Counseling and Discipleship (IBCD) in Escondido, California. Over the past several years, a large percentage of my cases have involved conflicts between parents and their adult kids. I've seen first-hand the very kinds of problems I've introduced here. I've also seen parents who seek to micromanage their adult kids, treating them as though they were still children unable to make mature choices for themselves. I've helped families in conflict over dating and marriage choices, over adult kids in trouble with debt or the law, and even over what the role of parents should be in the lives of their grandchildren.

The hours we've spent in counseling with real families like yours have been enriching to our souls. We're extremely thankful for them because we've seen the power of God's Word displayed in the lives of his people as they have gained confidence in his will and have experienced the blessing of his presence and wisdom. We trust that you'll experience the same blessing as you learn what it means to say with Elmer and with us, "Even though it is sometimes difficult, I'll never stop being a parent."

One thing I've learned through all of this heartache and conflict is that a book that comes at these issues from a consistently biblical point of view is desperately needed. Because we fully believe in both the infallibility of Scripture and the sufficiency of God's Word to equip us for every good work (2 Tim. 3:16–17), this book will probably be different from others you have read. This book is based on the assumption that Scripture is sufficient not only to tell us how to gain salvation, but also to help us establish wise, godly relationships with our own adult kids.

This book is unique in another way too: Rather than relying on a list of formulaic steps, it will point you to the cross and to the one Man who had a perfect Father, and who was a perfect Son. It's because of his incarnation—he actually lived in a normal family with a mom and dad, and brothers and sisters—that we can assure you that he has experienced every temptation you're facing now. It's because of his sinless life, the way he perfectly loved his heavenly Father and his family, that you have access into God's presence as a forgiven, justified child. It's because of his death on the cross, which paid the price for all your sins—not just the big ones but even the seemingly insignificant ways that you've loved yourself or your children more than you've loved God—that you can stand before your Father completely sinless and completely righteous. He's also your risen Lord who conquered death and the power of sin to free you from slavery to the old way of doing things. You can change because Christ is risen! And finally, the gospel message reminds us that Jesus Christ is now ruling as Lord over all, sovereignly superintending everything that happens in your life and in the lives of your kids. Jesus Christ has also sent the Holy Spirit to live in your heart and assure you that these struggles aren't all there is. You may be suffering deeply now, but there is more than this life to focus on.

While it's true that parenthood ends when we enter eternity, if you're a Christian you can be completely sure that God will never stop parenting you. He has promised never to leave you nor forsake you; he is your Father and that will never change. He will always protect you, provide for you, and pardon you. He is your merciful, everlasting Father. In this truth, you can rest and face the day with confidence. This world and these difficulties aren't all there is. There is a heavenly Father to whom you can address all your concerns and who bears you on his heart. (If you're not sure that you're a Christian, please turn to the back of this book to appendix C for clarification.)

# 1

# Is It That Time Already?

WHEN KATE LEFT for college she intended to study music, but her parents insisted on a premed track. By working very hard, she was able to major in music and also complete the premed requirements her parents preferred. But now she's a senior and faces a difficult decision. Her father insists that she continue on to medical school to fulfill his dream of her becoming a doctor and ensuring her financial independence. Kate on the other hand longs to be married and have a family. She's already met a fine Christian man and would like to get married when they graduate in May. To make matters worse, Kate was raised as a conservative Anglican and her boyfriend is a Baptist. Her father cannot bear the thought of his grandchildren not being baptized as infants, and therefore has forbidden Kate to marry her boyfriend unless he becomes an Anglican. Kate wonders if she should comply with her father's wishes and pursue medical school. She's confused about God's will and wonders if she's free to marry when her parents don't approve. What should she do?

Bill and Eileen have worked very hard to build a successful business. They have sought to give their children every material and educational advantage. While they enjoy very pleasant relationships with their twenty-four-year-old son, Pete, and their twenty-two-year-old daughter, Jane, Bill and Eileen are deeply concerned that their children aren't getting anywhere in life. Pete made it through three years of college studying to be a nurse, but now isn't sure whether he wants to continue. He has dropped out of school and is living at home, working part-time at a fast-food restaurant. Bill and Eileen are concerned that he's wasting time playing video games instead of planning his future. Jane's goal is to be a wife and mother, and she doesn't see any point in furthering her education. While she is definitely helpful around the house, her day isn't fully occupied. She spends hours on Facebook connecting with friends all over the country but has no marriage prospects.

Bill and Eileen love their children, but they wonder if they are enabling laziness. They can't understand why their kids aren't motivated to make something of themselves. "When we were their age we were full of drive and ambition. What is wrong with kids these days?" they wonder. Sometimes, after working long days, Eileen gets angry because it seems like her kids are living off her and Bill's labors without having to work hard for themselves.

Wayne and Kathy have five wonderful children ranging in age from ten to nineteen. While parenting has had its challenges, generally they feel exceptionally blessed. Their family is very close and each of their children seems to genuinely respect their parents. Recently, however, Wayne and Kathy have been troubled by changes taking place in their eighteen-year-old daughter, Danielle. Danielle has always been a compliant child and a great help with her younger siblings. Now, however, Danielle is changing, challenging some of her parents' standards in terms of clothing and entertainment. Also, Danielle wants to go away to college instead of following her parents' plan for her to take classes at the community college, while helping out at home. Perhaps most troubling, Danielle no longer wants to attend church with the family but is interested in trying out some of the more contemporary churches where her friends attend. Wayne and Kathy aren't sure what they should do.

In each of the stories above, parents and their adult children are in conflict. Kate is compliant and obedient but questioning just how far her parents' authority rightly extends into her adult life. Pete and Jane are typical twixters, living off their parents' labors and not really getting anywhere. Danielle is living at home but beginning to question her parents' authority. As each of these stories illustrates, people are complex and their relationships are often a tangled web, woven over decades. For this reason, none of these stories is black-and-white, and each requires wisdom from the Lord.

### Wise Living Is the Goal of Our Parenting

Most parents understand that childhood was designed to be a temporary season of training—a time to equip children to live as wise, independent adults. It is toward this goal that many of us have prayed and labored for years. Mothers and fathers understand that all too soon our little ones will be heading off to college, walking down the aisle, or simply promising us they'll call. Parenting is a temporary season of our lives, and it's one that we'll have to say good-bye to, perhaps before we're ready.

This brevity is God's design. It isn't merely cultural mores; it is part of God's creation order. From the very beginning, the Lord declared that sons and daughters would leave their parents' home and establish new homes of their own (Gen. 2:24). Even if our young adults don't marry right away, they're still expected to move beyond childhood and mature into adults as 1 Corinthians 13:11 says: "When I was a child, I used to speak like a child, think like a child, reason like a child; when I became a man, I did away with childish things" (NASB).

But brevity doesn't mean insignificance. This season of parenting is so significant that an entire book of the Bible is written about it. Proverbs is written as a training manual for parents to equip their sons and daughters to live as wise, independent adults in the world. "Our goal in training and discipling our children, is to bring them to maturity," one teacher writes. "If we are so blessed, they become self-governing and ready for adulthood long before it is time to release them from the home."[1] In the conclusion to his excellent book, *Shepherding a Child's Heart*, Tedd Tripp writes, "The parenting task comes to an end. We are no longer the on-site shepherds. That aspect of our relationship is done. This will be true whether they marry or just take their place as an adult in their community. God intends for it to be a temporary task."[2]

### Prepare Yourself for the Empty Nest

Does anyone really enjoy change? Even when our lives are fraught with difficulty, the difficulty we're familiar with always seems better than the difficulty we haven't known. Letting go of our role as parents, even if that role has become stressful, can be troubling and even frightening. Some couples have built their relationship around their children and now fear what might happen when they leave. What will we talk about if not the kids? Will our relationship be able to withstand this test? Do we even have a relationship aside from our children? Some mothers, after having devoted more than twenty years to training their children, don't know what they'll do with themselves when the kids are gone. One father writes, "For my wife who was a stay-at-home mom, the hardest aspect of dealing with our youngest child was the radical change in involvement. . . . To use my wife's own words, 'I went from first string involvement to being a bench player.' "

No one likes being replaced on the starting team. No one enjoys facing futility or obsolescence. None of us take pleasure in facing the truth that one very significant portion of our life's work has come to an end. None of us like change, particularly when the change means that our identity and relationships must be reshaped.

## It's Not Really an Empty Nest

It's easy to see that the strength or weakness of a marriage is a major factor in how parents deal with children leaving. If a marriage is strong, even though saying good-bye to kids marks the cessation of a very significant relationship, the spousal relationship can be sustaining and enriching during this trial. If, on the other hand, a marriage is weak and is built around the children rather than the parents, these good-byes can seem almost unbearable.

We know that if you're reading this book, you may think that it's too late for you to change the tenor and focus of your marriage. After all, you've been relating to each other in this way long enough to have adult children. Although a loving marriage might seem like a hopeless proposition to you right now, the Lord, who called you both together and who has made you both one, is able to revitalize and revive the love you once had. In fact, he's in the business of taking enemies (if that's what you've become!) and making them one. His love is so powerful that he has even taken the sin that separates the lost from his adopted family and "broken down in his flesh the dividing wall of hostility . . . that he might create in himself one new man in place of the two, so making peace . . . [and] no longer strangers and aliens, but . . . fellow citizens . . . being joined together . . . into a dwelling place for God by the Spirit" (Eph. 2:14–22).

Jesus Christ takes pleasure in making lovers out of those whose lives have been filled with hatred, suspicion, lack of interest, and boredom. Remember, if he's powerful enough to reconcile hateful rebels to a holy God, he's powerful enough to reconcile you and your spouse, no matter how many years it has been since you actually cared for each other. (See the "Resources for More Help" section for books on this topic.) In the meantime, even as you're reading this book, try to remember what first drew you to your spouse. This season of life after your kids are gone can be a wonderful time for romance. Now, with all of your history and shared experiences, your spouse can become your new best friend!

These years can also be a wonderful time for ministry together. You finally have time to serve the Lord and his church in ways you had only dreamed about. I have greatly enjoyed being able to take Caroline along with me for conferences and short-term missions trips without having to worry about kids back home. Caroline has also been able to pour herself into the lives of the younger women in our church and community, following the model in Titus 2:3–5.

We've come to realize that the term *empty nest* is misleading. When the kids leave, the nest is not empty because you are both still there. Furthermore, as your marriage relationship grows and becomes even stronger, your home can become a very special, warm place to which your adult children will want to return for special family events and holidays. And it can be a place where they can seek refuge in times of trouble. Empty nest? Hardly.

## Parental Control or Friendly Influence?

During the years when our children were yet children, we had the right and obligation to oversee every area of their lives. We determined how they were to be educated, chose their friends, and set the standard for their entertainment. We were the in-control parents, and they were to be the in-submission children. However, during this training process, the day-to-day control had to diminish, and our children were given more and more freedom to make choices and to learn from them. After all, the core of what it means to mature is the ability to make wise choices in real-life situations. Hopefully, as they taste success and failure, they gradually will learn to make responsible choices, rather than having to suddenly cope with the snares of independence and decision making when they move out.

Our relationship with our adult children changes as they age. Whether we like it or not, rather than fighting to maintain control, we should strive to change our relationship from in-control parents to respected friends.[3] If we want our children to mature into responsible adults, we've simply got to let them make their own choices and then learn from those decisions. We cannot (and should not) force them to follow our will—even when we know we're in the right. If a relationship of openness and mutual respect has been developed over the years, hopefully they'll seek and heed our counsel as people who know them well and have their best interests at heart.

Peacemaker Ministries[4] teaches the concept of having "passport" in the lives of those we are trying to influence. Just as we need a literal passport to gain the right to enter a foreign land, we need to earn the right to speak into the life of another adult (even our own child's). Of course, in the same way that we might be able to enter a foreign land by force if we had a big enough army, we may be able to get our adult child to comply with some of our demands through threats or manipulation. In cases like this, even though we may have won a battle, we're in danger of losing the war. Strong-arm tactics and dictatorial rule won't engender love and respect in adult kids. It will not win the hearts and minds of those we are hoping to persuade. Instead, it will likely have the opposite effect: the adult child will simply bide his time until he has the means to escape your control, or he'll give up in frustration and bitterness.

We gain passport with our adult child by treating him or her with love and respect. If we can patiently learn to listen rather than always demanding to be heard, as James 1:19 teaches, our child will know that we respect his opinion and his right to differ with our views. As one parent reported to us, "Our kids can have a lot of insight that can be helpful to me! I've learned to try to listen."

We lose passport when we nag, manipulate, and demand control.[5] When experienced parents were asked to share the main lessons they had learned in dealing with their adult kids, the most common answer was learning when *not* to speak. One wrote, "The greatest challenge has been not giving my opinion about things. I often have the urge to offer advice in order to help my children keep from making mistakes or poor choices." Another states, "The most challenging aspect in dealing with my adult children is to . . . remember that I am merely counseling. The kids don't have to do what I tell them."

We understand how difficult it is to learn to listen, especially when what's being said seems so immature and foolish. We can fight our impatience by remembering how willingly Jesus listens to us, and how foolish, weak, and sinful we would seem to him if it were not for his love.

## The Relationship Has Changed

Most Christians agree that when children marry they establish a new, separate family unit (Gen. 2:24) and are no longer under parental authority. But what about adult kids who remain single? Some Christian teachers and seminar leaders assert that adult children are to be absolutely subordinate to their parents until they marry. In contrast, while we believe that the Bible requires single adults to honor their parents, it also teaches them to be independent and responsible for their own choices.

Our Lord Jesus clearly portrays this change in his relationship with his mother in John 2. When she mentions a lack of wine at the wedding in Cana, Jesus, a young, unmarried man, replies, "Woman, what does that have to do with us? My hour has not yet come" (John 2:4, NASB). While Jesus loved and honored his mother, he was no longer subordinate to her. And because this example comes from the life of Jesus himself, we can be sure that his relationship with her was the supreme example of what it meant to be a godly child.

The concept of a single adult being responsible and independent is also found in John 9, where we find the Jews questioning the parents of the man Jesus had healed of blindness. Although they might simply have been trying to protect themselves, the concept of an adult child's personal responsibility is clear. Although it's reasonable to assume that they knew what had happened to him and that he wasn't a married man, instead of answering for him, they responded to the Pharisees' questions by pointing them toward their now-seeing son: "Ask him; he is of age, he will speak for himself" (John 9:21, NASB).

The Gospels are not the only place we see this concept. Numbers 1:3 indicates that those who were twenty years old and above were considered old enough to be numbered among the men of Israel and able to go off to war. Paul speaks of a child being "of age" in Galatians 4:1–2, explaining that an heir manages his own affairs once he is an adult and not under a guardian. Paul also describes the advantages of remaining single in 1 Corinthians 7:32–34.

> One who is unmarried is concerned about the things of the Lord, how he may please the Lord; but one who is married is concerned about the things of the world, how he may please his wife, and his interests are divided. The woman who is unmarried, and the virgin, is concerned about the things of the Lord that she may be holy, both in body and spirit, but one who is married is concerned about the things of the world, how she may please her husband. (NASB)

What is Paul teaching here? Simply that an adult may choose to remain single so that he or she may serve the Lord with undivided devotion. He does not say that the single adult must remain single to serve or please his parents, nor does he teach that a daughter must marry if that is what they wish. Paul's assumption seems to be that in their adulthood, singles are accountable directly to the Lord, which implies that they are independent of their parents, who in many cases were probably not believers. Certainly, there is no indication that Paul, though single, was subordinate to his parents. Some teachers claim that daughters are to be treated differently than sons and must remain under the absolute authority of their parents until they are married. But Paul gives a clear example of a single woman being fully given to the things of the Lord, which would assume a certain level of independence from her parents.

The Bible even gives examples of adult children taking a stand against their parents. Jonathan rightly stood against his father Saul by making a covenant with David and loyally defending him. When the twelve spies sent out by Moses gave their reports of the Promised Land, the people received the false report of the ten unbelieving spies rather than the report of Joshua and Caleb. Numbers 32:11 recounts the Lord declaring that none of the unbelieving men who were twenty or older would enter the land. This implies that a single, twenty-year-old adult was "of age" and responsible to make his own choices in life. He could not use the excuse that he was simply following in his parents' unbelief. Rather he had the duty to take a stand for the Lord by following Joshua and Caleb, even if this meant going against his parents who stood with the unbelieving spies.

Pastor John Piper wrote that the church must "sound the trumpet for young adults that Christ is Lord of their lives and that they are not dependent upon mom and dad for ultimate guidance."[6] Or as one astute twenty-four-year-old wrote of her understanding of authority, "Parents aren't the final arbiter of truth; God is, and it is with Him whom we all have to deal!"

## But Aren't Children Commanded to Obey Their Parents?

Some of you may be wondering about Ephesians 6:1 and the command for children to obey their parents. Doesn't this command extend even into adulthood? Or could there be a limit implied in it? Some parents might say that this command applies to children of all ages. But in light of the passages explained above, we believe that Paul is referring to children who are still dependent upon their parents and under their roof and authority, as opposed to those who are "of age."[7] The application of the commandment to older children, even those who are married, obliges them to honor their parents (Ex. 20:12) by showing them respect and helping them when they are in need (1 Tim. 5:4). (See appendix B for more on this.) However, they are no longer obligated to submit to them or obey them in all things.

It's a sad reality that some parents sinfully abuse their position of authority. Amelia was a woman in her early thirties who was still living with her parents and being courted by a fine Christian man. The catch was that the man's work was thousands of miles away from Amelia's family. Her parents refused to allow their daughter to marry this man, because they simply didn't like the idea of their daughter moving so far away. We advised Amelia that her parents were wrongfully trying to control her (Eph. 6:4), and according to Scripture, she was free to choose whether or not to marry.

In another case, Jorge, a single man in his early forties, was living with his divorced mother who objected to his desire to marry a godly, Christian woman he had been courting. She wanted him either to continue to live with her or to marry the woman she chose. Jorge's mother claimed that Ephesians 6:1 proved that her son would be violating Scripture to marry against her will. Jorge sought counsel from church leaders who convinced him that he was free to choose his wife. Today Jorge and his wife have a blessed marriage with dear, beautiful children. He and his wife are doing all they can to show kindness to his mother despite her opposition to their marriage.

The problem of parents refusing to let go and trying to control the choices of their adult kids is not a new one. In the sixteenth century, Martin Luther's father wanted him to be a lawyer, but Martin was determined to be a priest. Although the conflict between father and son was painful, every Protestant can be thankful that Luther went against the desires of his father and made his own choice. God used his determination to be his own man in marvelous ways that are still resounding through the world more than five hundred years later.

Like Luther, our young adults are responsible before God to make their own choices. They are responsible to choose their vocation, marriage partner, and place of residence. When our children were young the choices available to them were limited by our preferences. But now that they are "of age," they are free to leave our home and supervision, even if we believe that decision is foolish.

## We All Need So Much Grace

Every human relationship requires grace to survive. People living in close quarters will wrong each other. Parents become impatient and nag. Children sometimes are self-centered and unappreciative. We're tempted to think that our way is the only way. We're convinced that we really do know best. But our adult children are convinced of the same thing—they believe that they are the ones who know what's best. Every generation in our home is proud, selfish, and demanding. One parent reminded us, "Don't be surprised by sin! We are all sinners."

Yes, we're all sinners. This is the reason that we need much grace, and the good news is that we've been given grace upon grace in the person and work of Jesus Christ. As those who have been the recipients of such astounding grace from an infinitely holy and eternally wise God through our Lord Jesus Christ, we are compelled to show grace to one another and to fight against the selfishness, fear, and demandingness that threaten to engulf our souls. We're commanded to "be kind to one another, tenderhearted, forgiving each other." But how are we to do this? How are we to forgive those kids who have hurt us, or who are going against our wishes? There is only one source of power that will enable us to treat our adult children as we should. That power is the forgiveness and grace we've been given in the gospel. The end of the verse above tells us how to obey its command to love our adult kids: "just as God in Christ also has forgiven you" (Eph. 4:32).

## Let's Think More about It

Summarizing the main points of a chapter as soon as you've finished it is a good aid to help you to remember what you've read. You can write the answers to these questions in a journal or in the margins of the book. Either way, you'll be able to more easily recall what you've learned.

1.  What are some of the difficulties you're facing with your adult kids?

2.  Review the biblical foundation that we laid for saying that children who are "of age" are responsible for their own choices. What's your response to these verses? What do you agree or disagree with?

3.  If you're married, how did the concept of the nest not really being empty strike you? How would you rate your marriage at this point? Are there concrete steps that you think you should take to make your marriage sing again? What would they be?

# 2

# Before You Walk Out
# That Door . . .

CAROLINE AND I have some very special friends who have
ten children. The youngest is just starting elementary school
and the oldest is in his mid twenties. We have never known
a family that is so close and has so much fun together. Our
friends have trained their kids with great success. But what
has impressed us most is how well their older children have
transitioned into adulthood. Our friends started preparing
their children to be responsible, independent adults from
early adolescence. As these young adults have faced various
challenges and important decisions, their parents have not
tried to control or micromanage them but have waited for
their children to seek their counsel.

We had a relationship with each of our children that enabled us to openly discuss the things they were discovering and the events that were shaping their lives. We believe one of the key factors that enabled us to shape their hearts was the respect we gave them as they were maturing. When they questioned our rules or standards we explained our reasoning as we would to any questioning adult. When we asked our children why they continued to be open with us throughout their late teens and early twenties, they told us it was because we treated them as adults, respected their opinions, and gave them freedom as long as they acted responsibly. We knew we could no longer command and discipline them for disobedience. Our premise was that we tried to develop a biblical way of thinking throughout their lives, and when they reached somewhere around age twenty, our main role changed to that of counselor. . . . They trusted our counsel because we respected them and only spoke of absolutes when we could prove our point clearly from the Bible.

Their twenty-two-year-old son gave us his perspective on why his relationship with his parents remains so strong.

We had so much fun as a family! Family fun is not mere frivolity, but a vital means of building family culture and relationships. As children, we constantly visited libraries, camped for weeks on end, visited amusement parks, toured museums, played games, wrestled, and roughhoused. As I went through the teen years, they kept putting money in the bank of the relationship (of course, with young adults, literally putting money in the bank is always a good idea too!). One of the things I have really appreciated about my parents has been their openness to discussing ideas and differing viewpoints. They have never simply assumed I was wrong. They listened patiently and either kindly pointed out the flaws in my thinking or conceded that, while perhaps not what they would do, my actions or decisions were acceptable from a biblical standpoint.

## *Here Are the Things We Want You to Remember, Dear*

Christian parents understand that our job isn't merely to get our kids through the educational process. A high school or college diploma is not the goal. We've been entrusted with something far greater than being sure Susie passes calculus or Johnny stays out of trouble. We know that we are preparing them for the day when they will ultimately leave our home and our daily influence, the day when they'll be mature adults rather than grown dependents.

Here's how the apostle Paul summarized his goal for those he was discipling, his children in the faith: "The goal of our instruction is love from a pure heart and a good conscience and a sincere faith" (1 Tim. 1:5, NASB). We're working toward a higher goal than producing offspring that will make us proud (or at least not embarrass us). We're hoping that our children will come "to know and to believe the love that God has for us" (1 John 4:16) and will respond to this astonishing love with a life that is marked by a pure heart, a good conscience, and a sincere faith. These are our goals and they are as different from the goals of our secular neighbors as day is from night. We're planning for the future but it's not simply a future here in modern suburbia. It's an eternal future in the presence of the living God, rejoicing in the beauties of the Lamb slain before the foundation of the world. Here are some of the means that God may use to help us achieve these goals.

### 1. Teach Your Children the Love of God in Christ Jesus

Aside from the gospel, nothing else matters. Don't skim over that statement and assume that we're using hyperbole. We're not. No charts, stickers, earned privileges, 4.0's, or astronomical SAT scores will matter when our children stand before the Father and are asked one simple question: Who will pay for your sin? At that final moment, nothing else will matter. And the answer to that question has only two possibilities. Either our children will pay for their own sin in excruciating pain and suffering away from the presence of the Lord for eternity, or someone else will have paid for it for them. And even though, as a loving parent, you might be willing to pay it for them, you won't be able to because you'll have your own debt to reckon with. Only a completely righteous person is able to pay for the sins of another. Only Jesus Christ is able to bear both the responsibility of perfect obedience and the weight of God's just wrath against us.

Therefore, we need our children to learn that Jesus Christ came into the world to save sinners, people just like them. He didn't come to save the successful, the righteous, and those who don't need help. He didn't come to save those who fancied they could keep the law or obey their parents flawlessly. He came to save sinners. God's love for his children is so great that he generously gave his Son for them. *Convey this truth to your young adult.* Show him Jesus! This is our primary responsibility. If our children walk out that door without knowing that there is a love of incalculable worth being offered them, we have not said what must be said. We've missed the most important truth in the entire universe: Jesus Christ is preeminent and head over all things, but he died for sinners!

Perhaps right now you're filled with regret. Perhaps you're remembering all the times when a perfectly made bed or passing grade was more important than sharing the love of God with your kids. Perhaps this gospel understanding is something that's new to you, and you haven't really shared your faith with your kids yet. Our goal is not to make you feel bad. Our goal is to encourage you that it's never too late to say it. Maybe you've said it a hundred or a hundred thousand times. Say it again. "Jesus Christ died for sinners!" This is your primary calling.

## 2. Teach Your Children to Fear God and Live for His Glory (Deut. 6:5; Matt. 22:37)

Proverbs (the book of the Bible written to help parents train their children) tells us, "The fear of the Lord is the beginning of knowledge" (1:7).[1] Even if our kids know plenty of facts about the physical world, even if they are fluent in three languages, unless they love and worship the Lord, they don't know anything. They're still naïve.

Many young people from Christian homes are what the Bible would call naïve. Biblically speaking, being naïve isn't a compliment. It's a term that essentially describes those who are undecided between the wisdom and righteousness of God and the attractions of the world. The naïve young adult usually acts one way when around her parents and a completely different way when with her friends. The undecided, lukewarm fence sitter is sadly naïve. She doesn't understand that by failing to choose wisdom she has already chosen foolishness.

The first nine chapters of Proverbs contain extended appeals to young people to turn away from the foolishness of the world and to commit wholeheartedly to wisdom and to the Lord. Parents cannot make their children wise. We cannot force them to abandon their naïveté. What we can do is continually portray the beauties of the Lord, who is our wisdom and righteousness (1 Cor. 1:30). We can make clear the choice between wisdom and foolishness, joy and despair, and blessing and heartache. We can also pray. We can pray that the Holy Spirit will use our meager, faltering attempts as means to speak to their hearts.

## 3. Show Your Children How to Put Others Ahead of Themselves

Aside from the work of the Holy Spirit, we're all self-centered, aren't we? But because young people aren't as adept at masking their self-interest as we are, they seem even more so. The world reinforces this immature self-focus with its emphasis upon self-love and self-esteem (2 Tim. 3:2). Sociologist Jeffrey Arnett, speaking of trends among young adults, says that

> delayed adulthood is a new social phenomenon, which allows self-centered Americans even more time to focus on themselves while not being responsible for anything else or to anything else. This is the one time of their lives when they're not responsible for anyone else or to anyone else. So they have this wonderful freedom to really focus on their own lives and work on becoming the kind of person they want to be.[2]

In contrast with this world's self-centered, instantly-gratified, entitled frame of mind, the Lord Jesus delayed his experience of full joy until *after* the work he had come to do was accomplished: "For the joy that was set before him [he] endured the cross, despising the shame." Not until after the manger, the accusations, and the thorn and the hammer was he "seated at the right hand of the throne of God" (Heb. 12:2). He did not merely seek to please himself, but rather set an example by serving us (Rom. 15:2–3; Phil. 2:3–8). Young people need to be reminded that Jesus is not only their example of generous service but is also the Suffering Servant, who counted sinners as his brothers and sisters and pursued their joy before his own, granting his righteous record to those who believe.

Little babies, cute as they are, don't understand the concept of patient forbearance when their tummies growl. They only know they're hungry and they want food, now! A display of growth in maturity is the ability to put others' needs and desires ahead of our own. A young person who is living in a narcissistic, private world of video games needs help to see that he must focus on others if he is to mature. The last few months or years that your kids spend living at home may be your final opportunity to prepare them to live in community, whether their journey out the door leads them to start their own families or live with roommates in a college dorm.

### 4. Help Your Children Learn How to Communicate with Wisdom and Humility

Before our children leave us and enter into their own adult relationships, a growing competence in loving communication skills will be essential. Words are extraordinarily powerful. As Proverbs 18:21 teaches, "Death and life are in the power of the tongue," but these skills are sadly lacking among most young adults today. To verify this statement all one needs to do is watch fifteen minutes of any reality show. Our culture's young people have been well schooled in how to emote, demand, gossip, boast, and use profanity, but the skills of a gentle answer or loving confrontation are utterly nonexistent. Even those who have been taught sound communication tactics use words primarily to achieve their own personal goals, rather than to bless and serve others. Again, this self-serving speech is merely a symptom of the selfish bent of our hearts, and learning to speak in a grace-giving way is something we all, not just our kids, need to grow in.

But consistently gracious, gentle, and selfless speech is not a skill that can be learned as simply as learning a second language. We can teach our kids to say please and thank you in twelve different languages, but if their hearts are unfazed by the gracious life and words of Jesus Christ, their life and words will not be grace-filled. The Bible teaches that our words reveal deeper truths about us. They are either the fruit of hearts that have been transformed and humbled by grace, or they are the rotten product of hearts striving for control, dominance, and self-centered pleasure. Jesus himself poses this question, "How can you speak good, when you are evil?" He then answers it by diagnosing our problem with evil speech: "For out of the abundance of the heart the mouth speaks" (Matt. 12:34). Before our young adults' speech will be genuinely gracious, their hearts have to be gracious—and this gracious transformation only happens through the power of the Holy Spirit in response to the gracious preaching of the gospel.

We need to teach young adults the art of avoiding unnecessary offenses through quarreling (Prov. 16:19; 17:14; 20:3; 26:21) and careless or angry speech (Prov. 12:16; 13:3; 16:32; 21:23). They need to learn how to actively and carefully listen (Prov. 18:3; 20:5) and to build up each other with encouraging words (Prov. 12:25; 15:7; 25:11). And because sinners living in close quarters will inevitably clash, they'll also need to learn to resolve conflicts biblically (Rom. 12:18) by confessing fault, granting forgiveness (Prov. 19:11; Eph. 4:32), and gently confronting sin (Prov. 27:6; Gal. 6:1). But the motivation and desire to speak in these ways will only flow from the realization that they've been loved and forgiven even though their speech is wicked enough to condemn them (Matt. 12:37).

The best way for our children to learn these communication skills is by seeing them practiced in their own family, in the context of a daily, cross-centered life. Ideally you started speaking with them about Jesus' self-abasing, gentle, and welcoming words long ago. In that context, hopefully you granted them the freedom to admit their own sin and need, to speak their minds, to respectfully disagree with you, and to voice their doubts and confusion as you lovingly sought to understand them. But even if this perspective has been lacking until now, you still have a great opportunity to develop a gracious relationship with them by learning to speak to them as peers and friends, rather than subordinates under your authority.

## 5. Teach Your Children God's Design for Sex and Marriage

Lengthy sections in Proverbs are devoted to warning young people against the dangers of sexual immorality, while encouraging them to find sexual fulfillment within marriage (Prov. 2:16–19; 5:1–23; 6:20–35; 7:1–27). The desire for marriage often motivates the pursuit of adult maturity and responsibility. Research has shown that married men enjoy significantly more financial success than single men in otherwise similar circumstances (i.e., education and work experience).[3] Most assume this is because they are motivated by the desire to care for their families and have the support of their wives. Godly young people often marry at a younger age than most when compared with the culture at large, mostly due to a commitment to moral purity. Another reason may be that they are more mature than others their age. We should do our part to encourage this, teaching them not only sexual purity, but also biblical perspectives on manhood and womanhood, so that they can know the kind of person they need to become and the kind of spouse to choose.

## 6. Teach Your Children to Choose Their Friends Carefully (1 Cor. 15:33)

After the prologue, the book of Proverbs begins with an appeal to a young person to avoid foolish companions and not give in to peer pressure (Prov. 1:10–19; 29:25). "He who walks with wise men will be wise, but the companion of fools will suffer harm" (Prov. 13:20, NASB). The young person is also instructed how to be a true friend: "A friend loves at all times and a brother is born for adversity" (Prov. 17:17, NASB; see also 27:9–10).

## 7. Let Your Children Practice Making the Choices of Adulthood

While a teenager whose every choice is tightly controlled by her parents may seem compliant and submissive when living at home, she may be unprepared to make wise decisions when she is on her own. If your young person is still under your supervision, granting her the freedom to develop her own convictions, make her own decisions, and solve her own problems will help her avoid many pitfalls later when you won't be around to mitigate the consequences. As one wise dad wrote,

> One of the things we wanted our girls to learn was how to be problem solvers. So, when they came to us for help, we encouraged them to think through the matter themselves first and decide the best course of action on their own. Rushing in with the answer would have been easy for us but wouldn't have helped them in the long run.

We realize that relating to young people in this way may be distressing and difficult for many parents because our kids rarely come to exactly the same convictions and decisions that we do. While we agree that truth is not relative, that there really is evil and good, there are also areas where sincere believers may have differences of opinion. In these areas, we should grant our children the privilege of choosing their own path.

In light of our life and counseling experience, one of the biggest mistakes we have seen Christian parents make is overly sheltering their kids from the world. While we think that a certain amount of protection from evil influences is appropriate, especially when children are smaller, many young people from Christian families enter adulthood totally unprepared for the temptations they will face. Some, at the first breath of freedom, will run headlong into the world, yielding to the allurement of the forbidden.[4] Parents should give their children increasing responsibility and freedom as they get older, including the freedom to make some choices contrary to the ideals of the parents. One dad told us,

> As the children entered the early teen years, we told them that we considered them adults—immature adults admittedly—and we would grant them increasing freedom based on a demonstration of their increasingly responsible behavior. Of course, this didn't mean that it was easy to let them go. . . . Despite our focus on preparing our children for independence, when the time actually arrived for them to take long journeys from the nest, it was emotionally trying. For their entire lives, we were there, very actively protecting them, monitoring behavior and attitudes, and being the primary shaping influence of their thinking. Now they were facing influences beyond our control and developing independent opinions and making independent decisions.

### 8. Teach Your Children the True Value of Hard Work and Money

If our children are to be prepared for independence, they must learn to take care of their own material needs. The formula taught in Proverbs is hard work times skill produces wealth (Prov. 10:4; 12:24; 22:29). Those who are diligent in their work will prosper. Those who are lazy will go without (or they will try to return to their parents' home). Skill is also an important factor. An unskilled laborer will make less in a week than a highly skilled worker will probably make in a day. We should encourage our children to develop a godly work ethic and to acquire marketable skills so that their labor will be in high demand—so that they can "stand before kings" (Prov. 22:29).

On the other hand, some become so consumed with making money that they go to the other extreme. Our culture is filled with materialistic, self-aggrandizing schemes for achieving personal success. These self-destructive goals and the desires that motivate them amount to spiritual suicide according to the apostle Paul.

> Those who desire to be rich fall into temptation, into a snare, into many senseless and harmful desires that plunge people into ruin and destruction. For the love of money is a root of all kinds of evils. It is through this craving that some have wandered away from the faith and pierced themselves with many pangs. (1 Tim. 6:9–10)

Jesus put it even more plainly: "You cannot serve God and money" (Matt. 6:24). Before teaching our children the value of hard work and money, we need to live lives that seek the greater riches of an eternity with God. This inheritance transcends the value of the dollar, financial freedom, and vocational success. We need to remind them of the grace of the Savior who, "though he was rich, yet for [our] sake he became poor, so that [we] by his poverty might become rich" (2 Cor. 8:9).

The motivating factor behind godly hard work must be the generosity of Jesus Christ who knew what it was to eschew the riches of heaven, become poor, and then transfer all his riches to others. Although we should instill within our young adults an appreciation of the much-valued and wise Protestant work ethic, if we fail to teach them about true riches, we will have overlooked the most important truths about vocation and money. After all, "what does it profit a man to gain the whole world and forfeit his soul?" (Mark 8:36).

## Please Don't Go Out that Door Quite Yet . . .

Sadly, many of our children want complete adult freedom before they are ready to assume the responsibilities of adult privileges. Sometimes they leave in anger, immaturity, and rebellion. Other times they're just desperate to prove that they can make it on their own without our help. Although we understand the desire to prove one's independence, it is sad to see young people harm themselves by failing to take advantage of living at home while completing their education or vocational training. Ironically, many young men join the military to escape authority, while some young women get married to gain independence. These kinds of choices often result in a more demeaning and restrictive environment than they would have experienced by staying at home a little longer.

Of course, some young adults leave in order to escape a difficult home situation of abuse, neglect, or overbearing parents. "Fathers, do not provoke your children, lest they become discouraged" (Col. 3:21). We understand the desperation of a young man whose parents abuse him, or a young woman who is humiliated by an overbearing father. We know many young adults who have left their homes as soon as they turned eighteen, even though they weren't really ready to do so. Our hearts grieve that this type of scenario is all too common.

### Granting More Freedom May Persuade Your Immature Child to Stay a Bit Longer

We all need God's grace and wisdom in managing our children's transition to adulthood. While we have the right to maintain certain expectations of any adult who is living in our home, these expectations need to be adjusted according to the age and maturity of our kids. Like all adults, young adults hate being nagged and micromanaged. Most of all, they hate being treated like children and long to be respected as the adults they are becoming. They also strongly desire the approval and encouragement of their parents, which means parents need a great deal of patience! This forbearing patience and understanding is only possible when we're remembering how patient God has been with us.

The Bible reminds us that people are different and need to be treated according to their maturity level (1 Thess. 5:14). While the age of twenty may be a general guideline for judging when a child becomes an adult, it's certainly not universal. Don't assume because your first child was on her own when she was twenty-three that the others will follow the same timetable. Some kids have high-paying, full-time jobs and can support themselves when they are in their late teens. Others still need significant help with their social skills in their mid-twenties (though such kids typically don't realize it).

It is very hard to watch your children leave the nest before they are ready, but forcing them to stay is not an option. They may need to gain maturity through the hard process of reaping what they have sown (Gal. 6:7). It may be that, like the Prodigal Son, they will need to spend some time in the far country where they will be humbled before God and grow to appreciate their family. If your child has left your home too soon, hope remains that the Lord will still work to draw him or her to himself. Keep praying!

## Is It Time to Say Good-Bye?

Parents in our culture generally let their kids go way too soon, allowing them to make all of their own choices in terms of entertainment, relationships, and clothing in their early teens. On the other hand, many Christian parents tend to control their young adults too much by making every decision for them. Finding a proper balance is not easily discernable.

The good news is that we don't have to try to sort things out by ourselves. Much like our young adults, we need wisdom too. Here's a promise that you can cling to: "If any of you lacks wisdom, let him ask God, who gives generously to all without reproach, and it will be given him" (James 1:5). You have a *generous* heavenly Father who is more than willing to bestow wisdom upon you when you ask. Perhaps you'll have to ask more than once—this might be a six-month or two-year request—but the Lord, the fount of all wisdom, is able to enlighten your heart to correctly say either "good-bye" or "please stay." He may do this directly through his Word or through a combination of other factors like particular circumstances, the counsel of others, or even this book. We can never know exactly how, but he will give you the wisdom you need for every day as promised.

## Let's Talk More about It

1. What do you believe about the gospel? Is it really good news to your soul? Have you sought to communicate the good news to your young adult or is Christianity simply a set of moral rules to them?

2. What work remains in order to prepare your children to leave home? What is your strategy for finishing the job?

3. If you're not sure whether your kids should leave home or stay a while, try keeping a journal of your prayers for wisdom. Record what you've prayed about and the ways in which God seems to be guiding you. Remember that the Lord never guides us to disobey his Word.

4. Summarize what you've learned in this chapter in four or five sentences.

# 3

# You Say Good-Bye,
# but He Says Hello

EDDIE HAS ALWAYS been a really nice kid. He is easygoing and friendly. Eddie, however, is thirty years old and is not making much progress in life. His official designation is "student," but he only completes a few courses each year and hasn't quite decided on a major at the local community college. He works part time at Starbucks, making just over minimum wage plus tips. Because Eddie still lives with his parents, he has enough money to keep his car running, eat out with his girlfriend, and own the latest cell phone. But last month he had to borrow money from his mother, Lois, to pay for his car insurance. She lent him the money, reasoning that if Eddie can't drive, he can't go to school and work. Eddie's father, Jeremy, is getting fed up with the situation. Why does he have to work fifty hours a week while Eddie sits around half the time doing nothing? Jeremy frequently makes snide and sarcastic comments when he sees Eddie playing video games or using Facebook on his iPhone. Occasionally, Jeremy gets angry and threatens to kick Eddie out of the house, but Lois intervenes and the matter is dropped. Jeremy is ready to say good-bye.

After hearing about the problems in other families, Paul's parents were thrilled when he completed college in four years, even though it wiped out most of their savings. After graduation, Paul moved back home and spent the summer hanging out with friends and surfing the net. His parents understood that Paul wanted a break after finishing school, but now they want him to get a job. But Paul doesn't want to get tied down by a career at this point in his life. He plans to work in construction for a few months in order to save some money so he can spend a year traveling in Europe. His parents don't like the idea of their son bumming around after they spent eighty thousand dollars in educating him. Paul likes saying hello when his parents foot the bill.

## The Era of the Twixter

Scenarios just like these are being played out in thousands of homes. Social scientists have noticed that more young adults (those between eighteen and thirty years old) are putting off the responsibilities of adulthood. *Adultolescence* is the term that best describes this postponement of adulthood into the thirties. This phase is characterized by identity exploration, instability, focus on self, feeling in limbo, and a sense of limitless possibilities. These characteristics are accompanied by transience, confusion, anxiety, obsession with self, melodrama, conflict, and disappointment.[1] Others have called this the "Peter Pan Syndrome" because these kids just don't want to grow up. The percentage of American children, or "kidults," in their mid-twenties living with their parents has nearly doubled since 1970.[2] Some never leave. Other adult children who had previously left are coming back after completing college[3] or because of economic or personal problems. One survey reports that only 16% of mothers and 19% of fathers say their children (ages eighteen to twenty-five) have reached adulthood. Even more alarming is that their kids don't dispute it: only 16% consider themselves to be adults.[4] Articles dealing with the complicated relationships between adults and their grown dependent children have appeared in many publications including *Money*[5], *The New York Times*, and *The Wall Street Journal.*

This trend is not unique to America. *Time* points out that other nations are facing similar challenges. The British call them "kippers"—Kids In Parents' Pockets Eroding Retirement Savings. The Australians call them "boomerang kids"—you throw them out but they keep coming back. Nor has the church escaped this phenomenon. Christian leaders including John Piper, Albert Mohler, and others have written articles about how this issue affects the church.[6]

The tension experienced in many families is that our young adult children want full adult privileges and freedoms without assuming adult responsibilities. They expect mom to do their laundry and cook their meals while dad works to put a roof over their heads. But if parents try to impose expectations upon them they angrily protest that they are no longer children. The phenomenon of the twixter occurs because parents allow it to. After all, who wouldn't want free room and board?

### Valid Reasons for Twixters to Live at Home (for Now)

In discussing the twixter phenomenon, we're not saying that there aren't good reasons for some to postpone their good-byes. There can be many blessings, both familial and financial, when a young adult lives with his parents. They can enjoy mutual family fellowship and a growth in relationship as adults relating to one another as friends. Young adults may also significantly contribute to the family dynamic,[7] while parents can be a source of guidance and accountability. Because it takes time to attend a four-year college or to learn a trade[8], most are not prepared to start either a family or a career.

A young adult may defer leaving home while he's completing his education, establishing a business, or saving for marriage. Temporarily living at home can save tens of thousands of dollars and allow a student to complete his education more quickly than if he had to provide his own room and board. Small out-of-pocket costs for parents can translate to huge advantages for their adult children. This follows the wisdom of Proverbs: "Prepare your work outside and make it ready for yourself in the field; *afterwards, then,* build your house" (Prov. 24:27, NASB, emphasis added).

Some young adults are not physically or mentally able to take care of themselves. David and Leah have six grown children, but two—Peter and Rachel, who are in their early thirties—have significant disabilities that prevent them from working or living on their own. As David and Leah get older, they wonder who will take care of Peter and Rachel when they are gone[9], since they will never be able to function as responsible adults. Along these same lines, adult children may choose to stay at home in order to help take care of their aged or disabled parents or other family members (Matt. 15:5–6; 1 Tim. 5:4).[10] Thirty-five-year-old Ralph has a good job as a computer programmer but has never married. He is happy to live with his parents who are in their late seventies and is a great help to them, especially since his father has recently suffered a stroke.

Children also may move home because of extraordinary circumstances such as a married daughter who has been widowed or abandoned, or a son who has lost his job and needs a place to stay during a time of transition. Kate and Tom knew that after their marriage they should leave and cleave, but when Kate was injured in an auto accident she couldn't take care of herself let alone their three small children. Temporarily moving in with her parents allowed Tom to go to work and for Kate and the kids to get the care they needed.

## Home for a Season and a Reason

"The plans of the diligent lead surely to abundance, but everyone who is hasty comes only to poverty" (Prov. 21:5). If a young adult is living at home, there should be a clearly agreed upon purpose and plan for his stay. Failure to do so will probably result in conflict and will tempt him to aimlessly drift through life following the course of least resistance. For instance, the student should have a plan to graduate in a reasonable period of time, with progress toward that end being a condition of remaining in his parents' home. The daughter who chooses to live at home while waiting for marriage should stay busy. She should get a job or further her education in case she has to take care of herself. The son who had to come home because of financial trouble should have a plan to eliminate debt and to accumulate savings in order to regain his independence. In each case, clearly defined seasons and reasons will significantly help to avoid conflict and misunderstandings.

This does not mean that every young adult living at home must leave by a certain time. As long as she is productive and there is a mutual agreement for her to remain at home, a daughter (or son) can be a welcome member of the family.

## *There Is a Time and a Reason for This Season to End*

While many young adults have valid reasons for staying home, some are wasting time and their parents' resources while they wander aimlessly. David Brooks, a columnist for the *New York Times*, argues that there has been a generational shift toward this kind of behavior over the past fifty years.

> People who were born before 1964 tend to define adulthood by certain accomplishments—moving away from home, becoming financially independent, getting married, and starting a family.
>
> In 1960, roughly 70 percent of 30-year-olds had achieved those things. [But] by 2000, *fewer than 40 percent* of 30-year-olds had done the same. (emphasis added)

These goals drastically set apart those in previous generations from those in "the decade of wandering," which Brooks describes earlier in his column as "frequently occur[ring] between adolescence and adulthood":

> During this decade, 20-somethings . . . take breaks from school. They live with friends and they live at home. They fall in and out of love. They try one career and then try another.
>
> Their parents grow increasingly anxious.[11]

When we allow our young adults to flounder in self-gratification year after year, we're not doing them any favors and may actually be enabling immaturity and selfishness. For instance, when we consistently provide for them financially, we're removing the impetus that would naturally impel them to establish a career of their own. Proverbs 16:26 states, "A worker's appetite works for him, for his hunger urges him on" (NASB). Need compels work. When we supply the car, a cell phone, a room, and food, there is little incentive for some young people to acquire a skill and work hard. They are able to enjoy the fruits of prosperity without having to sacrifice.

In former generations, college used to be a short time of transition to adulthood after which the graduate would begin his career. But now, many twixters stretch their college experience over decades as they wander aimlessly through myriads of choices and opportunities, all on their parents' dime. Jeffrey Arnett, a developmental psychologist at the University of Maryland, describes the period between ages eighteen to twenty-five as a kind of sandbox where young adults build castles and kick them down. They experiment with different careers, knowing that none of it really counts. After all, "this is a world of overwhelming choice."[12] This self-centered narcissism is at the heart of what drives this lost generation.

Many people in their late twenties can't make a decent living, often earning barely above minimum wage.[13] Contributing to this inability to support themselves, many young adults believe that they shouldn't pursue a career unless they know they will love it and it will further their pursuit of "self-actualization." Many of them fail to understand that even those who have very satisfying jobs rarely love them all the time. In addition, the real world (away from mom and dad) doesn't always afford us the opportunity to endlessly pursue our dream job (Prov. 28:19). Bill Gates and Steve Jobs are famous because they're unique. Most people don't strike it rich or get to do what they love all the time.

Because many young people have wholeheartedly imbibed this counterfeit and immature perspective of work, they never follow through when the going gets tough. They believe that work is supposed to be fun, and they only do what pleases them. They would do well to learn that work is called *work* because it isn't always enjoyable and it involves effort.

While they lethargically pursue their dream job, some young adults are critical of their parents for being workaholics. Perhaps children have seen how their parents have foolishly sacrificed relationships and leisure activities for their careers. In response, they have wrongly harbored a general resentment and censure of people who are devoted to their jobs. While we have seen the destruction that idolization of work can cause, we've also seen the destruction of sloth and narcissism. In their effort to avoid the error of materialistic fixation on job and career, these young people have tragically squandered years of their lives.

A Christian perspective on labor (whatever form it might take) must include a profound joy that originates in the understanding that our work is for the Lord, who labored and languished on the cross for us. We work out of deep gratitude, whether our job is boring, strenuous, or dull. Even seemingly meaningless jobs have meaning because we are working for our Savior. Paul commands us to have this perspective and explains where our true reward is found: "Whatever you do, work heartily, as for the Lord and not for men, knowing that from the Lord you will receive the inheritance as your reward. You are serving the Lord Christ" (Col. 3:23–24).

If our young adults are Christians, their lives have meaning. They are not living futile, dead-end lives, no matter what kind of work they do. Rather, they are living the life that the Lord has laid out for them—a life that might seem insignificant right now but has great eternal consequence. We need to teach them the honor of honest work and the joy that comes from knowing that our lives count for the Lord. Although their employer on earth might do little to inspire them, their real employer is the Lord Christ.

The belief in the dream-job fantasy of fun, fun, fun can only be sustained because our young adults have been given the means to live well without having to work hard. With this entitlement mindset, they fully expect others to take care of their financial needs. Financial independence, once a mark of maturity and a goal to be pursued, is now reality for only half of those ages eighteen to twenty-nine.[14] Among those who are financially dependent on others, most of their support comes from dad and mom, either directly through cash payments or indirectly through free room and board. Others seek help from the government, fully expecting hardworking taxpayers to supply every need and desire. Some are perpetual students in a constant search for grants and funding for never-ending learning and education. Many have not yet experienced the challenges and blessings of earning, budgeting, and saving in order to create a decent lifestyle.

In addition to feeling entitled, many of our young adults are financially irresponsible. They often work only enough to pay for their desired level of discretionary spending. Because their parents pay for their essentials, they are free to spend more on entertainment and the latest technology. They typically eat out more, take more exotic vacations, drive nicer cars, and own nicer gadgets than their parents simply because their parents haven't yet said good-bye. Watch the ads that are aimed at our young adults. Advertisers have a real stake in keeping them in a "tractable, exploitable, pre-adult state—living at home, spending their money on toys."[15]

If we fund the majority of our young adults' wants and desires, they will come to believe that instant gratification is the norm. For most of them, the concept of saving is utterly foreign. As a result, they are often deeply in debt, and yet they continue to spend money on short-term gratification rather than eliminating their debt and saving for the future (Prov. 22:7). Many expect their parents to make their credit card and car payments if they are facing financial trouble. While we understand that sometimes our children have emergency needs, it is both unloving and unwise for us to repeatedly bail them out. The Bible teaches that we are responsible to work hard to provide for ourselves rather than looking to others to take care of us (2 Thess. 3:10–13).

In addition to being characterized by financial neglect, young adults also tend to view marriage as a low priority. Instead of marrying and having a family, many of our sons and daughters indulge in uncommitted relationships and even illicit sex. Because they've eschewed the responsibilities of work and saving for a family, and because they abhor commitment, wanting to keep all their options open, young adults marry much later than at any time in our history. Since the past generation, the median age of a first marriage has risen by five years.[16] If you ask them, most young adults will say that they want to marry some day, but first they want to enjoy their freedom.

It's not hard to see that there are significant problems with this trend. First, it is one more manifestation of self-focus. Rather than using one's life and energy to love God and to love others (Phil. 2:3–4), our young adults are pursuing their own selfish pleasures. Dr. Al Mohler, president of Southern Seminary, warns that "the delay of marriage will exact an undeniable social toll in terms of delayed parenthood, even smaller families, and even more self-centered parents."[17] Furthermore, this disturbing delay of marriage sadly does not mean the postponement of sex. "The fact that they are marrying late means they have more sexual partners than previous generations."[18] In counseling with young people, including many from Christian homes, we have been amazed at how many are sexually active. Many see nothing wrong with what they are doing even though Scripture plainly teaches, "Marriage is to be held in honor among all, and the marriage bed is to be undefiled for fornicators and adulterers God will judge" (Heb. 13:4, NASB).

## Sometimes Love Means Saying Good-Bye

Beth and Steve can't agree about whether to help their nineteen-year-old son, Chip, who has moved out of the home and has started his own struggling small business. Chip wants to buy a fancy sports car. Steve argues that they can afford to help him and is excited about their son having flashy new wheels. Beth is concerned that material things have come too easily to Chip, and that it would be better for him to enjoy the finer things in life after he has earned them himself. After all, Steve was only able to afford his dream car a few years ago after spending many years working hard building a career.

As parents of young adults, we understand that saying good-bye can be very difficult. Like you, we struggle with letting go, and after the challenges some of us faced during those teen years, our young adults are now easy to have around. The irrevocability and the emptiness of finally saying good-bye sometimes seems overwhelming, perhaps most of all to a mother who has poured her very lifeblood into her children. And then there's always the question of what life will be like when it's just you and your spouse at home. The loneliness, the marked change of season, and the inevitability of aging are both frightening and heartrending. Even though it doesn't feel like it, and even though our hearts want to help and continue to parent our adult children, sometimes the most loving thing you can do is to say good-bye.

## Let's Talk More about It

· · · · · · · · · · · · · · · · · · · · · · · ·

1. How do you feel about saying good-bye? What stops you from doing so? Have you sought counsel from your pastor about what steps you might take as you seek to make this break?

2. We mentioned some good reasons to let your child remain at home for a season. Do any of those reasons apply to your situation? If not, have you formulated a plan for your son or daughter to leave your home?

3. Do you see any of the destructive tendencies that we mentioned in this chapter in your adult child? How have you inadvertently reinforced the selfishness and narcissism of this present age?

4. Would you encourage Chip's parents to help him buy the sports car? Why or why not? What kinds of goodies have you purchased for your adult child that he would not have been able to afford otherwise?

5. Summarize what you've learned in this chapter in four or five sentences.

# 4

# Saying Hello to
# Pleasing God

KEVIN AND JULIE have three adult sons. Two of them are living independently after completing their education and settling into careers. In sad contrast, their middle son, Mark, is still living at home at the age of twenty-seven. After high school, he started a few classes at the local junior college but dropped out because he was tired of school. He played drums in a band that he formed with some friends, but they never got any paying gigs. A few years ago, Mark moved out and got an apartment with some buddies. But last year, he returned home not only broke, but with over thirty thousand dollars in credit card debt. Kevin couldn't stand to see his son paying over 20 percent interest, so he paid off the credit card on the condition that Mark pay him back some day. Mark has a minimum wage job and works about twenty hours a week to pay for his gasoline, car insurance, and entertainment expenses. He also spends a lot of time surfing, playing video games, and hanging out.

To complicate matters further, Kevin and Julie discovered that Mark was addicted to prescription pain medications that he had been acquiring illegally through the internet. At the insistence of his father, Mark went to a doctor to seek help. After the appointment, Mark told his father that the doctor had given him a prescription to help wean him off the pain medicine. Kevin has been giving Mark fifty dollars in cash each week for several months to pay for his medication. Now Mark claims that the doctor has ordered a three-month period to detoxify from his prescription, during which he won't be able to work. Mark wants his dad to make his car payments and to meet his other expenses. When questioned about the details of his doctor visits, Mark insists that that information is private.

## A Priest Who Said Good-Bye to God

The unintended errors made by Kevin and Julie in the story above are being repeated in countless homes across our country. In fact, we're sure that some of you resonate with their story. But our country at present isn't unique. The truth is that these kinds of stories have been told for thousands of years. Three thousand years ago, God's servant, Eli, made critical mistakes in raising his sons. In fact, his mistakes were so serious that he's not remembered for being a wise and godly priest, but rather as the classic biblical example of poor parenting. Although it's likely that Eli's poor parenting didn't start when his children became adults, the narrative doesn't begin until his sons are already young men, active in daily ministry as priests. This sad figure in Israel's history is the quintessential example of a father who chose to please his sons rather than God and lost everything he cherished as a result.

In case you're unfamiliar with his distressing story, Eli served as God's priest in the days of the judges, along with his sons, Hophni and Phinehas (1 Sam. 1:3). The Bible uses very negative language regarding these two boys. They are described as "worthless men; they did not know the Lord" (1 Sam. 2:12, NASB). These young men took what they wanted from the people's sacrifices, rather than following God's law, and then bullied faithful worshipers who protested (1 Sam. 2:13–16). They also abused their pastoral authority by committing sexual immorality with the women who served at the tent of meeting (1 Sam. 2:22). Serious as these actions were, they were simply the fruit of hearts that had an utter disregard for the holiness of the Lord, their work, and their father's position. Their continual rebellion and indifference invited the judgment that they eventually received (1 Sam. 2:17).

You might be wondering what Eli did when he heard the reports about his sons' behavior. He didn't just remain silent and play dumb but repeatedly, verbally admonished them.

> "Why do you do such things, the evil things that I hear from all these people? No, my sons; for the report is not good which I hear the Lord's people circulating. If one man sins against another, God will mediate for him; but if a man sins against the Lord, who can intercede for him?" But they would not listen to the voice of their father. (1 Sam. 2:23–25, NASB)

Eli was fully aware of his sons' actions, and he knew that they were not only in the wrong but in danger of the Lord's judgment. He certainly nagged them and criticized them, but he did not restrain them and ultimately both he and his sons paid the price.

Eli may not have been able to change the hearts of his evil sons by pleading with them, but as the chief priest he should have removed them from the priestly service to the Lord. By allowing them to abuse their priestly office, Eli was guilty of enabling their sin and thereby complicit in their abuse of the Lord's worship and his people. Instead of judging them as the law commanded (Deut. 21:18–21), Eli allowed them to continue serving as judges in Israel. Therefore, the Lord severely judged Eli along with his sons. "And I declare to him that I am about to punish his house forever, for the iniquity that he knew, because his sons were blaspheming God, and he did not restrain them" (1 Sam. 3:13).

### Was Eli's Failure Really That Bad?

Why did Eli let his sons get by with such horrible evil when it was his responsibility to correct and control them? The Lord got to the heart of the matter very clearly:

> Why do you kick at My sacrifice and at My offering which I have commanded in My dwelling, and *honor your sons above Me*, by making yourselves fat with the choicest of every offering of My people Israel? Therefore the Lord God of Israel declares, "I did indeed say that your house and the house of your father should walk before Me forever"; but now the Lord declares, "Far be it from Me—for those who honor Me I will honor, and those who despise Me will be lightly esteemed." (1 Sam. 2:29–30, NASB, emphasis added)

The Hebrew word translated *honor* literally means "treat as weighty or significant." Eli's sin was that he treated his sons as more weighty or important than the Lord. He was so concerned with maintaining the peace that he didn't have the courage to do what the Lord required him to do.

60

## Yes, And Eli Isn't the Only One

Eli was not the only failed parent in the Bible. His protégé Samuel also had adult sons who did not follow in his ways (1 Sam. 8:1–3, 5). Later, King David's failure to deal justly with his adult children when they were guilty of rape and murder (2 Sam. 13) ultimately led to civil war in Israel. Later when David's son Adonijah attempted to snatch the kingdom from David's appointed successor Solomon, it was said of him that "his father had never crossed him at any time" (I Kings 1:6, NASB).

Eli was like many parents today who observe the sins and weaknesses of their wayward sons and daughters and fail to act. Like Eli, such parents may nag their children: "I am sick and tired of seeing you sleep until noon and then lie around the house all day wasting your time. Get up at a decent time and get a job or go to school!" Or, they may plead with them: "You know that it is wrong for you to sleep over at your boyfriend's house. How can you do this to your father and me?" Or they may threaten them: "This is the last time I am going to pay for your car insurance and cell phone!" or "If you come home drunk one more time, we'll kick you out!"

Many parents feel hopeless. We know that our words don't have the desired effect, and yet we don't know what else to do. We plead, cajole, and threaten, but when push comes to shove many of us just keep on providing food, shelter, transportation, and money. In response, our kids learn to tune out the nagging and easily disregard us.

While parents cannot be held responsible for the sins of their independent adult children, they are responsible for what goes on under their roof. When dad and mom, like Eli, become enablers of a sinful lifestyle, they inadvertently dishonor the Lord and share in the sin and guilt of their kids, even though that's the farthest thing from their minds.

## *We're All a Bit Like Eli*

We know that the words you just read were probably difficult for you. We didn't say them to merely make you feel bad. We desperately want to give you the courage to make difficult but godly decisions about how to interact with your young adult that may be living sinfully in your home. Many of us have never received any teaching about these issues. Others feel weak and confused, wondering if it's even Christian to force young adults to live responsibly. We feel entrapped by our love and hope for our children, and yet we know that the Lord is asking us to choose to serve him first.

More or less, most parents today, living three thousand years after Eli, share his sinful motivation. We honor our children above the Lord. We may even be tempted to turn a blind eye to their sin because we want to avoid conflict. We fear that our kids might get into even more trouble if we were to force them to leave home. We can't stand the thought of them suffering deprivation. We wonder what would happen if they had to live on the street. What would happen to them if we told them they had to choose between right and wrong? What if they chose wrong? [1]

We understand the heartache and confusion that you may be feeling, but allow us to speak bluntly out of a deep care for the next generation and your Christian testimony before them. When we refuse to do what the Scriptures require of us and allow our children to live an ungodly lifestyle, we are not doing so because we love our children (see Prov. 13:24). We are supporting their sin because we love ourselves more than we love them and their souls. We don't want to feel bad, we don't want to face conflict, and most of all, we don't want to suffer loss. Year after year we go on lying to ourselves, nagging our children, and hoping for the best even though we refuse to obey the Lord.

"Perhaps she'll change on her own," we idly dream. "Maybe this time he's not lying about doing drugs. I don't want to humiliate him by insisting that he get tested." Perhaps Eli thought the same sorts of things. Perhaps he hoped that if he wasn't too hard on his boys, they would appreciate all he'd done for them and change their ways. But they didn't. They looked at their father as old and weak and they paid the price for their folly.

All day, every day, we make choices. We choose whether we're going to love ourselves or our neighbor. We choose whether we're going to honor our children or the Lord. We know that the choices we're pushing you toward may be very difficult for you, but we want you to know that these are not choices you make alone. Your Savior was tempted in the very same ways.

> For we do not have a high priest who is unable to sympathize with our weaknesses, but one who in every respect has been tempted as we are, yet without sin. Let us then with confidence draw near to the throne of grace, that we may receive mercy and find grace to help in time of need. (Heb. 4:15–16)

In the garden of Gethsemane, your Savior was tempted to forego the wrath God was about to pour out on him, but instead, he walked all the way up that hill to save our souls. He knows what it's like to be tempted to do what feels comfortable and what will make others love and respect you. He understands the pain of losing a relationship and of risking it all for the sake of righteousness, and yet, he persevered for your sake. Because he sinlessly offered himself up for you, you can be confident that when you cry out to the Lord for help, he'll hear you. You can call on him right now, and he'll hear and answer you. Why? Because, if you're his, he has paid the price for every moment you lived like an Eli or his sons, and because he has transferred his perfect record of always pleasing

God to you. You can pray and know that he'll hear and answer because he's not like us. His love is completely unselfish and he always keeps his word. Go ahead. Pray to him now. He'll give you the strength you need to do the right thing.

## How You Can Begin to Say Hello to Pleasing God

Although we don't live in an agrarian society and few (if any) of us have much experience with donkeys, most of us know how stubborn they can be. Donkeys aren't fazed by pleading, threatening, or even whining and nagging. What a donkey understands is action as Proverbs 26:3 says, "A whip is for the horse, a bridle for the donkey, and a rod for the back of fools" (NASB). The whip and the bridle motivate him to do his job.

A young adult who is foolish (lazy, disrespectful, immoral, etc.) will not be persuaded by parental nagging and whining. It is only decisive action which will get his attention. We can't spank a twenty-year-old, but we can stop paying for her things and take away our car, cell phone, or credit card. We can establish requirements as a condition for remaining in our home and we can evict her if she refuses to follow reasonable rules.

Although it might seem harsh and unloving, taking action like this may be the very means that the Holy Spirit will use to get ahold of her heart. The Lord may use our simple acts of faith, our attempts at consistent discipline, as the means he will use to deliver her from a lifetime of foolishness and heartache. Perhaps saying hello to pleasing God and saying no to her will be the most loving and kind thing we can ever do for her. "Discipline your son [and daughter] while there is hope, and do not desire his death" (Prov. 19:18, NASB).

Parents don't always have to actively chastise their irresponsible children. Often the best thing for us to do is nothing. Sometimes love looks like taking a step back and allowing them to experience the fruit of their choices. Galatians 6:7 reminds us not to be deceived because, "God is not mocked; for whatever a man sows, this he will also reap" (NASB). It's easy to imagine that Eli was concerned about how his sons would provide for themselves if they weren't allowed to be priests any longer. Many parents can't stand to see their children experience the consequences of their foolishness (cars being repossessed, utilities being cut off, bankruptcy, homelessness, or even imprisonment). If we continually step in to "protect" our children from the consequences of their wrong choices, we may be guilty of honoring our children above the Lord by standing between them and the chastisement the Lord is bringing upon them. The Psalmist reminds us of how God uses affliction to draw wayward people near to himself: "Before I was afflicted I went astray, but now I keep Your Word" (Psalm 119:67, NASB). Remember that the prodigal son only came to his senses when his circumstances were so bad that he longed to eat pig food. Seeing our children in a far country, foolishly wasting their lives, breaks our hearts, but this may be the very instrument God uses to bring them to himself (Luke 15:11–18).

One parent, who understands this truth, writes,

> As adults, our kids stand before God and live with their choices. That's very freeing for us since so many parents feel guilty and responsible for their children's poor choices. Instead, we've learned to examine ourselves to see that we've done whatever is appropriate according to the Scriptures . . . and then we rest in the understanding they are adults over whom God is sovereign.

## God Always Blesses Our Simple Acts of Faith

What follows are two true stories about parents who decided to say hello to pleasing God and good-bye to their foolish children. Of course, not all stories end in this way, but we've seen enough of them to know that this kind of ending is certainly possible. But even if your story doesn't look like it's going to end like this, we know that God always blesses our simple acts of faith, either by granting us more faith and time to grow in perseverance, or by opening our eyes to the joys of walking by faith alone.

After Rob graduated from high school, his dad, Rudy, gave him an opportunity to go to a local college while living for free at home. Each morning Rob would leave the house and would return late in the afternoon. After the first semester Rudy asked to see his son's grades. Rob claimed that there were various administrative problems, which made his grades unavailable. This went on for weeks until finally, after much investigation, Rudy discovered that Rob had quit attending classes early in the term and had failed all of his classes. Instead of going to class, Rob had been spending all day in the library watching movies and playing games on his computer. Because this event was a repetition of deceptive and lazy behavior that had been going on for years, Rudy told Rob that he had to move out and find a way to take care of himself. Rudy suggested that Rob might consider spending some time in the military. Rob, assessing his own situation, decided to visit his local recruiter and joined the Air Force. After very successfully completing his first four years, Rob decided to make the Air Force a career.

Steve, age nineteen, appreciated his parents, but was tired of their rules. He just wanted to be a normal young adult like his friends instead of having to be accountable to his folks all the time. After Steve arrived home late one night with alcohol on his breath, and it was discovered that he bragged about smoking pot on his Facebook page, his parents knew that they had to lay down the law. Either Steve would agree to live by the family rules, or he had to move out. Steve decided that his freedom was what mattered to him most, so he rented an apartment with some of his friends. Several weeks later, however, he came back to his parents seeking their advice. One of his roommates didn't pay his share of the bills and Steve had to make up the difference. Furthermore, another roommate was a total slob, leaving his things everywhere and eating other people's food. While Steve likes his independence and takes pride in his new job, he has realized that all of his pay is going toward paying for his living expenses. He would like to gain some skills to get a better job, but he doesn't have time to work full-time and go to school. He is thinking of moving back home if his parents will have him back. Could it be that he's another prodigal son who has been given the privilege of experiencing the consequences of his choices? Will he also become a wise son?

## *Saying Yes to the Lord and Hearing His Yes in Return*

We know that much of what you've read in this chapter has been difficult. We want you to walk in faith before the Lord and make the right choices for your adult children. Perhaps right now you know that you need to make some serious decisions. May we encourage you to not delay in doing so? Our hearts are so self-deceived that it's very easy for us to tell ourselves that someday we'll take care of what we know we should do now. Eli probably told himself the same thing. But if someday never comes, our children remain habitually foolish.

We'd like to leave with you a thought of hope for the future. Because we serve such a powerful, sovereign God, we believe that you're not reading this book by accident. Perhaps you purchased it or received it as a gift, but regardless, we know that God has providentially arranged for you to read it. You can have hope that God will continue to work in your life and perhaps, through the decisions you make right now, he'll work in the life of your beloved child too. Perhaps you've realized that you've honored your sons or daughters over the Lord. Perhaps you think it's too late for you or for them to change. But remember that our God is the God who brings death to life, transforms unbelieving hearts to faith-filled obedience, and grants new mercies every morning! Perhaps this day will be that day of transformation for you and your child. Why not ask him to grant you grace to help you in your time of need right now?

## Let's Talk More about It

1. Do you see any correlations between the story of Eli and your situation? What are they? Can you think of any reasons why Eli allowed his sons to act the way they did?

2. The Lord said that Eli honored his sons above him. What does that mean? In what ways can parents be guilty of honoring their kids above the Lord? Have you done that sort of thing with your kids?

3. Do you think that there are changes you need to make with your children that would better reflect your determination to please God rather than your children? Are there people in your life to whom you can go for counsel? Can you make an appointment to do that right now?

4. What would a truly loving action look like in the life of your child? Ask the Lord to give you the grace you need right now to love your children more than you love having them around, being at peace with them, or being able to provide for them.

5. Summarize what you've learned in this chapter in four or five sentences.

# 5

# You're Welcome to Stay, But . . .

MARTY AND ANN dearly love their twenty-one-year-old daughter, Susanna. She is vivacious, cheerful, friendly, and usually very helpful around the house. But Susanna is in a time of transition. She can't decide whether she wants to resume her general education studies at the local community college or get a full-time job. Currently, Susanna works about fifteen hours a week and divides her remaining time between home and her boyfriend, Nick. Nick is putting himself through college and has at least three more years to go, which means marriage isn't an option for the near future. Marty and Ann have almost no conflict with Susanna, but they are still concerned that she isn't really moving ahead in life. They wonder what they can do to gently nudge her forward.

## *The Difficulties of Deciding to Stay*

Even under the best circumstances, adult kids living with their parents will face many challenges. These challenges are normal and simply part of the discomfort everyone feels when their relationships change—even when the change is the result of the longed-for maturing process.

One of the primary areas of conflict between us and our adult kids will occur simply because they are twixters. They're literally *in-between* independent maturity and dependent childhood. Undefined, in-between roles are hard on us all, parent and child alike. Although they're in what will hopefully be the final phase of their transition to adulthood, they are still dependent on us for some necessities. And even though they're usually very glad to have the help (sometimes too glad!), they also feel uncomfortable with having to rely on "mommy and daddy" like they did when they were young. They see their friends, many of whom have moved out, gotten married, or started their careers, and they feel like there is something intrinsically wrong with them. They feel like babies or losers. Because they're probably already highly self-critical, any criticism from us (especially criticism that reinforces their negative self-assessment) won't be well received. Adult kids are usually sensitive to feeling controlled or micromanaged by their parents; even if what we're saying is reasonable and we speak respectfully, it's likely that they'll be offended.

On the other hand, we're easily frustrated by a child who wants all the privileges of adulthood but avoids the responsibilities that adulthood necessitates. Perhaps we've seen other parents whose children are perennial students or loafers, and we've sworn that our kids wouldn't end up like that. Or, perhaps we envy other parents who seem to have more time for themselves, and we wonder when our time in the sun will come. When we nurture these self-centered thoughts, we're tempted to overreact to the normal difficulties of living with another adult. We might be tempted to micromanage their day or fly off the handle if we see them on the Internet or watching TV. We'll be extra sensitive when they're inconsiderate and leave their stuff all over the house, and they'll seem unappreciative and self-centered to us.

The dynamic of living with an adult child is inevitably a difficult one, no matter how much you love each other or how glad you are to be together. Because we're sinners, we easily see the speck in our kids' eyes while being completely unaware of the log that is in our own (Matt. 7:3–5). For this reason, clear, agreed-upon rules for life together are so necessary.[1]

## What Should I Expect from My Non-Christian Child?

We recognize that if our children are not believers, it's impossible for them to produce Christian fruit. But through common grace even a non-Christian can learn to work hard and live productively in a community. We should not be less supportive of our children who are not Christians in terms of their education and interests. Nor should we lower our household standards to a level that would displease the Lord.

## Some Ground Rules that Will Help

If our children are living on their own, both financially and physically, we have almost no control over the choices they make. Even so, we should seek to develop an open friendship with them, so that they will be open to hearing our wise counsel when they ask for it. On the other hand, if they are still dependent upon us, whether they live at home or not, we have both the right and the responsibility to expect certain things from them as a condition for our ongoing support.

Having expectations is not unreasonable, nor are we babying them by requiring certain behaviors. Much like an employer or teacher has certain expectations that must be met so that the relationship can continue unhindered, parents also must set expectations and make them known. As we said in the last chapter, we actually have a God-ordained responsibility to avoid supporting our kids' misbehavior and laziness. Laying out these expectations is both wise and loving.

### Expect Them to Be Productive

We know from experience how frustrating it is to live with kids who think that a schedule is something for old people who don't have a life. When our kids stay up until the wee hours of the morning, sleep until noon, and then lie around on the couch watching TV while we work, it's hard to avoid nagging and feeling like they're taking advantage of us. Disagreements over the proper use of time will erupt if we haven't set out clear, reasonable guidelines beforehand.

God's good design for us is that, like him, we work hard six days so that we can enjoy his rest on one (Ex. 20:9–10). God himself has built the need for scheduling into the very fabric of our lives by giving us day and night, seasons and years. If all we had was day and it never changed, it would be very difficult to feel motivated to accomplish anything. But because we've got days, seasons, and years, and because we know that there are certain tasks that must be accomplished before the winter comes, we're motivated to work. God has built these motivators into our lives as a good gift to us. Jesus acknowledged this when he said, "We must work the works of him who sent me while it is day; night is coming, when no one can work" (John 9:4; see also John 11:9; 12:35). On two different occasions Paul wrote that we should make the best use of our time because the days are evil and there are people who need to see the gospel

72

in our lives (Eph. 5:15–16; Col. 4:5). The psalmist knew the importance of intentional scheduling and wise discernment about productivity when he penned, "So teach us to number our days that we may get a heart of wisdom" (Ps. 90:12).

Rather than seeing a schedule as enslaving or as thwarting their creativity, our kids need to embrace it as the good means God has given, so that they might know the joy of accomplishing much for him (Prov. 21:5). Although vacations and rest are enjoyable, a directionless life of laziness will result in nothing but heartache.

> A little sleep, a little slumber,
>   A little folding of the hands to rest,
> Your poverty will come in like a vagabond
>   And your need like an armed man.
> . . . . . . . . . . . . . . . . . . . . . . . . . . . .
> Poor is he who works with a negligent hand.
>         (Prov. 6:10–11; 10:4, NASB)

These instructions are so vital to both our natural and spiritual well-being that Paul wrote,

> For even when we were with you, we used to give you this order: If anyone is not willing to work, then he is not to eat, either. For we hear that some among you are leading an undisciplined life, doing no work at all, but acting like busybodies. Now such persons we command and exhort in the Lord Jesus Christ to work in quiet fashion and eat their own bread. (2 Thess. 3:10–12, NASB)

If our children are lazy and refuse to work diligently, they are in effect stealing. In light of the great generosity of the Lord, we are to stop stealing and work hard—not simply to line our pockets but to be generous with others like he has been with us (Eph. 4:28).

We recommend not allowing your child to live at home if she will not work as hard as her parents do. The nature of her work may be flexible—it may include a combination of paid employment, education/training, volunteer work (i.e., church or charity), and helping around the house. One father who sensed that his twenty-year-old son was not spending his time wisely required him to do something productive for at least fifty hours per week and to keep a record of his labors if he wanted to keep living at home. The number fifty was based on the dad's forty-plus-hour workweek, and the additional time he spent working around the house. Young adults living at home should do an adult share of the housework, rather than expecting mom to cook and clean, while dad does all of the home repairs and yard work.

## Expect Them to Be Financially Responsible

When our kids reach adulthood they should start paying for their own personal expenses. If your child is a full-time college student, you may choose to pay for most of her necessities so that she can focus on her education, but she should still work part-time to pay for personal expenses, such as a cell phone and entertainment. If your child is working full-time, he should pay a fair share of household expenses, while saving for the day when he'll be able to be on his own.

If a child is living extravagantly and foolishly incurring debt, he should not be allowed to live at home. This might seem counterintuitive, but he'll never learn how to control his self-destructive impulsivity if you're continually bailing him out and enabling his foolish lifestyle. One twenty-one-year-old told us that he had learned that "nothing kills work ethic and discipline more effectively than the welfare state of parental indulgence."

As we have already seen, Scripture teaches that debt is to be avoided (Prov. 22:7; Deut. 28:44; Rom. 13:8). Except in times of extreme emergency, we shouldn't lend money to our children and especially not for discretionary items and expenses. Matt's twenty-six-year-old daughter Diane came to him wanting to borrow three hundred dollars to go to a wedding that weekend in Las Vegas. Matt realized that Diane couldn't afford the trip because she had not planned ahead and had spent her limited earnings on clothes and eating out. Matt decided that it would be wrong for him to give her the money. When Diane accused him of ruining her life and being selfish, he simply replied, "I have not purposely harmed you. You made choices of how you wanted to spend your money. These choices are the reason you're unable to go to the wedding this weekend. I love you and hope that you'll learn to spend your money more wisely and to save for the days when you want to do something special."

### Establish Reasonable Moral Standards

If our children wish to enjoy the benefits of living at home, we'll need to insist that they live by the standards of our household. Drunkenness (Prov. 20:1; 23:29–35; Eph. 5:18), substance abuse, and sexual immorality (Heb. 13:4) must not be tolerated, whether they take place inside or outside the house. We need to tell our kids that it isn't simply a matter of our wanting to control their lives but of our desire to live a life that will be honoring to the Lord, who has so loved us. We need to explain that if we tolerate these kinds of behavior we would be indirectly financing and enabling behavior that drove our Savior to the cross.

### Having Said All That . . . Don't Micromanage Them

We have already mentioned that the greatest mistake made by many parents occurs when we treat our adult children as if they were still very young. In response you might be thinking, "Yes, but if he acts like a child, shouldn't I treat him like one?".

We have heard of young adults who had to seek adult permission to leave the house during the day and had to be home by 10:00 at night. Certainly this kind of micromanagement is almost always inappropriate and won't do anything to help our kids grow in their ability to make mature choices.

We want to help our young people understand the difference between our negotiable house rules and timeless, biblical standards. For example, we can insist that any child living in our home is forbidden to watch pornography on television or on the Internet. This is clearly a biblical command that cannot be compromised. There are many other issues, however, in which we have the option to choose our own standards. In these cases, we should recognize that our children may not adopt identical standards. For example, some families choose to not subscribe to a cable television service. Some won't even own a TV. They may also choose to only attend G-rated movies. Others may have very strong feelings about having a glass of wine or beer. Many families also have very specific standards for how they will dress or whether they would swim at a public pool or beach. As our children get older we must give them leeway to establish their own standards for house rules on issues such as these. The chief exception is when their viewing or listening habits could influence or offend others in the house (i.e., younger siblings), in which case they would have to be careful not to undermine the standards and preferences of others.

## Living in Community in the Home

Our children will probably spend the rest of their lives living in community, whether it be with their own families or with roommates, and every community has certain expectations regarding contribution and courtesy. Our young adults should speak respectfully to us (Ex. 20:12; Prov. 20:20; 30:17) and make efforts to get along with other family members (Prov. 18:6), treating them with kindness (Phil. 2:3–4). Of course, we should show the same respect and courtesy to them.

Andrew, age twenty-three, was very busy with school, work, and his friends. His mother never knew when he was going to be home, and when he eventually arrived, he would retreat to his room and watch TV while working on his computer. Finally his mother, Diane, had to confront him. "You are not a child," she said, "but I am not running a boarding house. We don't expect you to be here at any particular time, but we would appreciate the courtesy of knowing when to expect you back and when you plan to share meals with us. Also, we'd like to have at least one dinner a week together as a family. Is there a night that would work for you?"

Nothing is more important for living in community with others than trust. Because we are not only family members, but hopefully also members of Christ's body, we are commanded to "put away falsehood . . . [and] speak the truth with [our] neighbor, for we are members one of another" (Eph. 4:25). People living together are like a body, and each individual acts as a part of that body. We need to work together, which can only happen when we can trust each other.

## What about Church?

Parents with adult kids living at home express a variety of strong opinions on this question. Many say that anyone living under their roof is expected to join the family once a week in worship. Other parents allow their adult children to choose the church they attend, as long as it is evangelical. This approach shows respect to their adult status, while also keeping the expectation that those living under the parents' roof honor the Lord through

77

church attendance. We also know parents who had required their children to attend church as minors but did not force them to attend once they were adults—even if they remained in the home. Their thinking is that if their unbelieving children are forced to attend, they would be exasperated (Col. 3:20) and all the more turned off to the things of God (Matt. 7:6). Those who come to worship should do so willingly and with joy. From these various perspectives we've concluded that this is a matter of personal conscience on the part of parents.

## Failure to Meet Expectations Must Result in Consequences

Why do people generally obey traffic laws? They fear the consequences of getting caught. Can you imagine how people would drive if traffic laws were not enforced? We would be afraid to go on the road.[2] In the same way, house rules that are not enforced will be ignored. The peace of many of our homes is shattered by the verbal battles between our adult kids and us. We believe that parents can virtually eliminate nagging by following through on specific consequences for failure to comply. Here are some examples that might help you to create fitting consequences.

Mack was having problems with his twenty-two-year-old son Seth who would come home late at night when everyone else was asleep. Mack would get up early the next morning to find every light in the house on and the front door unlocked. Mack would then charge into Seth's bedroom and chew him out for wasting electricity, leaving the house exposed to burglars, and being an immature, self-centered son. Seth, offended at having his manhood challenged, would react in anger, and a knock-down, drag-out argument would ensue. Their relationship was rapidly deteriorating.

Life changed when Mack decided to employ a different tactic. Instead of fussing at Seth, he implemented a system of fines. For example, if the front door was left open overnight, Seth had to pay his father a fine of fifty dollars, plus one dollar for each light left on. Seth agreed to this new regimen, preferring the potential economic cost to the shouting matches. Being treated with respect as an adult helped Seth to remember his responsibility to the household, and his dad never collected a dollar.

In another case, Paul had agreed to pay his parents three hundred dollars per month as his share of the household expenses. But Paul was forgetful and would have to be reminded several times before finally paying his rent. Paul's parents got increasingly frustrated with his lack of responsibility and consideration and would let him know just how they felt. Finally, Paul's dad decided to treat Paul more as a landlord would treat a tenant. If Paul were renting an apartment and forgot to pay on time, the apartment manager would not get personally offended and fuss at him. Instead Paul would be charged late fees and ultimately be evicted. Paul's parents told him that he was responsible to pay his rent by midnight on the fifth of the month or he would be charged an extra twenty dollars per day until he remembered. Paul's folks made a bit of extra money in the first few months, but Paul, who is pretty tight with his cash, soon learned to make his payments on time.[3]

Once when we shared these examples with another couple, they complained, "This wouldn't work with our daughter because she doesn't have any money." We then asked, "So how does she pay for her transportation, entertainment, and cell phone?" We recommended that they make a list of everything they are giving their daughter which could be taken away as possible consequences for failure to meet basic expectations. Anything that you are providing can be removed or repossessed, including access to the family vehicle, cell phones, the Internet, and television. The question wasn't whether this couple had sufficient leverage, but whether they would have the courage to deal with their daughter.

Some parents may object that disciplining a young adult through financial penalties, taking away privileges, or creating extra work is demeaning. We have found that young adults strongly prefer consequences to nagging and scolding. We also believe that such consequences reflect how the real world works. If you don't pay your apartment rent on time, the manager doesn't nag you. Instead he makes you pay a late fee. If you break the traffic laws the police officer doesn't scold you, he calmly writes you a ticket. If you break the traffic laws several times, the government will take away your driving privileges.

## For Their Sake, Follow Through

Most parents with wayward adult kids have made many threats, but few have carried them out. They have backed away from ultimatums, allowing the pattern to continue and their kids to never reach adulthood.

Often discipline fails because both parents are not of one mind. While mom seeks to establish and enforce high standards, dad undermines her efforts by letting the kid off the hook. Mom thinks dad is ruining their child by being too tolerant. Dad believes that he is the more loving parent and that mom is driving their child away through harshness. Young adults become masters of manipulating divided parents.

Discipline is hard work and is often unpleasant. "All discipline for the moment seems not to be joyful, but sorrowful; yet to those who have been trained by it afterwards it yields the peaceful fruit of righteousness" (Heb. 12:11, NASB). But, we continue to discipline our children in the hope that God will work in their hearts to make them wise.

An adult child who will not live by our rules cannot be allowed to stay in our home. Sometimes your child will try to make you feel like the bad guy for forcing him to leave. Or she may protest that she doesn't like being treated as a child. You should make it clear that every adult has choices to make. As the parent you have the right to set standards for your own home. Your child has a choice of whether or not to stay. She can agree to follow your rules and continue to enjoy the benefits of being under your roof, or she can say that she is unwilling to submit, thus making her decision to leave. If she wants total freedom she also needs to learn to take care of herself.

We know that we've given you quite a bit of information to think through in this chapter. We hope that you'll go back over it now and pray about those areas that are pertinent to your child continuing to live with you. Our goal in giving you these guidelines is simply to help you live a peaceful life with your child and to help him become the mature young adult that you're longing for him to be. We know that for some of you the steps we've recommended will be very difficult. That is why we're encouraging you to get good, godly counsel from your pastor or trusted friend and to cry out to God for the courage to do the best, most loving thing for your young adult.

## Let's Talk More about It

1. Of the areas we've mentioned to address with your kids, which ones are most important for you? When will you speak to him or her about it?

2. It would probably be wise for you to make a list of your expectations if your young adult plans to continue to

live with you. (See appendix D at the back of this book for some sample expectations in the form of a contract, which you can refer to or use yourself.) Don't forget to include concrete, easily understood consequences for failure to acquiesce to these expectations. After a time of prayer—perhaps even a week or two—ask your young person for an appointment and sit down and share them with him. Tell him that he doesn't need to agree to them immediately, but that you would like to have an answer within the next forty-eight hours or so. In the meantime, don't nag him or try to push him to make a decision. Simply pray and await his answer.

3. Summarize what you've learned in this chapter in four or five sentences.

# 6

# Thanks, I'd Like to Stay, If . . .

ELAINE, AGE NINETEEN, lives at home while working full-time at a daycare center. One day she may want to go to college, but for now she isn't sure what she wants to study. Elaine doesn't pay rent, but she does take care of her personal expenses. Elaine has been frustrated recently by her mother's attempts to micromanage her life. Elaine has a curfew of 11:00 p.m. every night of the week. Her mother, Sophia, reads her email and superintends her Internet usage. She insists that she must approve any movie Elaine attends. Occasionally Sophia makes Elaine take a drug test. What frustrates Elaine most is that she has never done drugs or given her mother any reason to mistrust her. Furthermore, Sophia is constantly nagging Elaine to be more helpful around the house.

Two nights ago Elaine came home at about 10:30 p.m. after spending some time with her friends from work. When she entered the house her mother started berating her for not having noticed the dirty dishes in the sink and for leaving her empty soda can in the living room the night before. Elaine just sat and took it, but inside she was seething. She is sick and tired of being treated like a nine-year-old. Even though she'd like to remain at home, she has decided that she is going to have to find a way to get out of her parents' house as soon as she can.

## Staying Home, from Their Perspective

The previous chapters have dealt with the difficulties parents face with their adult kids who live at home. We've also tried to help you see what reasonable requirements look like. Now, it's time for us to look at our role as parents and how we frequently make mistakes that contribute to the conflicts we have with our kids. In this chapter, we'll outline what they may reasonably expect from us.

Like our children, we're sinners. We assume that you agree with that statement—at least superficially. Our children are sinners because we've reproduced after our own kind. Simply put, they're sinners because we are. They're selfish, self-centered, and stubborn because we are. And even though we know that this is true, it's very difficult to see when we're in conflict with them. We're often guilty of the same selfishness, pride, and self-righteousness that they are. It seems self-evident that because we're older and wiser, and because we've sacrificed so much for our kids, the conflict in our home must be their fault. We forget that we fall into sin as readily as they do.

In Matthew 7:5, Jesus taught that before we can remove a speck from our brother's eye, we must first take the log out of our own eye. Pride blinds us not only to our own sin but also to the true struggles of others. And just as you wouldn't entrust your eyes into the hands of a blind ophthalmologist (no matter how much experience he had!), our kids won't feel comfortable trusting our correction of them when we're blind to our own sin, inconsistencies, and failures.

Humility is the fruit of the Holy Spirit's work in our hearts as he convicts us of sin and overwhelms us with reminders of our unmerited blessings. Humility is that quality of Jesus' life that enabled him to deal gently with sinners because he was tempted in the same ways they were (yet without succumbing to sin). Humility caused him to empty himself and become like us—to share in our weakness—to bear with our frailty. Look at how he is described by Zechariah and later Matthew: "Behold, your king is coming to you, humble, and mounted on a donkey, and on a colt, the foal of a beast of burden" (Matt. 21:5). He is the one who is "gentle and lowly in heart," and because of this humility we can come to him and find "rest" for our souls (Matt. 11:29). When we quiet our souls before his throne, seeing ourselves as we are, while at the same time seeing the great grace he has bestowed upon us, we can deal with our adult kids gently, admitting our own failures, and trusting in his mercy. Humility is the eyewash we need to use every day.

### Humbly Convey Clear Expectations

One of the primary conflicts between parents and their adult children occurs in the area of unclear expectations. Parents expect certain things from their kids and, when they don't comply, conflict arises. We're all guilty of assuming that others should be able to read our minds, which means we'll all gain by being clear in explaining exactly what we mean.

Unclear expectations are almost always unmet expectations because it's impossible to comply when compliance hasn't been defined. For example, if we simply tell our son that we want him to mow the grass, we'll probably be very dissatisfied with the results. Because our expectations haven't been made clear, the mowing of the lawn probably won't get done when we'd like it to.

On the other hand, if we're too exacting or demanding, we'll be guilty of micromanaging. Rather than saying, "Go outside and mow the grass now!" and expecting our child to drop everything, we can communicate that we expect the grass to be mowed by 5:00 p.m. every Saturday. This demonstrates both respect and trust. We're showing him that we respect that he has other things to accomplish and that we trust that if we give him the opportunity, he'll be responsible to comply. In framing our expectation in this way, he can figure out when he wants to get the job done and he'll be able to see that we're treating him like an equal rather than a subordinate.

Similarly, we may require a daughter to spend fifty hours a week in productive work, allowing her to choose which fifty hours she works. If she chooses to stay up very late and gets up at noon, as long as she gets her hours in and doesn't disturb others, she has met the expectation (and shouldn't be nagged). Again, this will show her that we respect her ability to manage her life, and we understand that she may choose to live it differently than we would. Respect for others and willingness to let them make their own choices is the fruit of humility.

One young woman told us that the primary parental error she'd seen was when parents

> continued to treat their adult children like young children . . . not allowing them independence or autonomy, while it is tacitly assumed that any and all of their choices are less than responsible and wise. While sometimes their choices

are indeed less than wise, many times the choices are the prerogative of being an adult (e.g., sleep schedules, money management, personal style, etc.). This is not to say that parents can never say anything, but usually parents err in the other direction.

A mom concurs: "Let go of micromanaging. The lion's share of your responsibilities as a parent has been completed. For the most part, it's now time to watch God's grace at work."

### Making It Really Clear

If there have been conflicts in the past about expectations, it's probably a good idea to put our concerns in writing. Although it might seem like an odd thing to do with our own child, a contract is a means by which expectations are recorded so that future disputes can be avoided or resolved. Adults frequently enter into contracts with one another, and it is a sign of respect when you enter into one with your child. We should remember that the rules of engagement for times of war are best written during times of peace.

Parents should include their adult kids in the negotiation process of defining expectations, rather than laying down the law without opportunity for input or discussion. They should also be willing to include in the contract what their children can expect from them. A starting point that demonstrates humility and respect is to have the young adult write down what he believes his parents should expect of him. In response to his list, his parents could then sit down with him and work through any changes they think need to be made.

Continuing in our desire to treat our adult kids with humble respect, we also strongly suggest that the list of expectations be shorter rather than longer. Remember that the Lord was able to summarize all his expectations of Israel in ten very easy-to-remember commandments. A lengthy list of requirements conveys that our kids can't be trusted to make proper decisions on their own without our managing it. This is not the fruit of humility which esteems others as "more significant" than themselves (Phil. 2:3). There is a sample contract in appendix D.

## Have We Mentioned This Before?

Did we already mention that young adults hate to be nagged? Before we tell our adult child something, we should ask ourselves, "Does she already know what I think?" If the answer is probably yes, then humble respect for her and for her ability to remember and think through the situation would dictate that we refrain from saying it again. Nagging will always damage a relationship because it is not the fruit of humble respect. It is the fruit of pride and impatience. Our children will perceive it as disrespectful—because it *is* disrespectful. Similarly, comparing our adult child with her siblings, the children of our friends, or even yourself when you were her age will only serve to alienate her.[1]

## Humility Speaks Little and Listens Much

We all need to learn self-control in the areas of our speech and our anger. As James wrote, we are to be "slow to speak and slow to anger" (James 1:19, NASB). Slowness of speech and anger is another fruit of humility—of remembering all that Jesus did to save us when we didn't listen and raged our hearts against him. He is the humble One, and if we're growing in humility, it's only because his life is flowing in us.

Although there are times to speak very strongly like he did, most of the time we should do all that we can to avoid quarreling (Prov. 17:14; 20:3). Because we're commanded to love our brother—even when our brother is our adult daughter—we must avoid sinning against her in our speech. It is never loving to vent our anger or speak hatefully to anyone. Sometimes we should simply walk out of the room and wait until we've remembered how loved we've been by Christ and how gentle he has been with us.

Our angry, proud words are so significant that our Savior likens them to murder (Matt. 5:21–22). The soul physician, James, helps us understand the motive behind these words. He tells us that we fight and quarrel because we desire something badly enough to kill for it (James 4:1–2). What is it that we want so badly that we're willing to sin to get it? Sometimes, we selfishly want our children to make us look good or for them to make our lives less difficult. Proverbs warns that a man who has no self-control is like a city with the walls broken down (Prov. 25:28). We need the fruit of self-control because we are in union with Christ (Gal. 5:22–23). Again, it is his self-control, love, and discipline that will enable us to control ourselves when we're tempted to give our kids a piece of our minds.

Because we're sinful and proud, the majority of us are poor listeners. We're accustomed to doing most of the talking while our kids listen to us. Listening is an easy way to demonstrate that we are sincerely interested in them as human beings. Careful listening demonstrates humble respect for their opinions and perspectives. Our soul physician, James, encourages us to be "quick to hear" (James 1:19). That means that we're to be right there, leaning forward, tuned in, eager to listen when our child speaks. This is a very difficult thing to do because listening involves not only effort and skill but also love and humility. "The purpose of a man's heart is like

89

deep water, but a man of understanding will draw it out" (Prov. 20:5). If we don't see ourselves as being both sinful and flawed as well as loved and welcomed, we really won't give a fig about what our child (or anyone else for that matter) thinks. Instead we'll be focused on getting our ideas out there and making our kids understand and obey. We'll never be the understanding parent who draws out the deep plans in our child's heart until the humility of Christ permeates our own hearts.

One mom we know pleads with parents, "Listen! Listen carefully!! Listen over and over. Persevere in loving them and in communicating with them. Be willing to recognize that sometimes you get it wrong." This kind of humble listening occurs only when we refrain from interrupting or correcting our adult children. Our home should be a safe environment where we are all free to express our ideas and opinions without fear, even if they are contrary to others' beliefs. As one young adult asserts,

> When a child becomes an adult they are free to think as they are inclined, and they should have the right to respectfully disagree with their parents. I think that the root of a lot of the problems that I had with my dad was because I didn't agree with him on some point. Parents need to let their adult kids disagree with them and not take it as a shot to their pride. . . . They should be open to the fact that they raised a new person, not clones of themselves.

Because our children are no longer children, we must realize that we cannot force them to agree with us. Instead we may seek to persuade them of the truth with the help of the Holy Spirit. When our adult kids question our house rules, humility teaches us that we should be willing to hear them out with an openness to reconsider our position.

Many parents of young adults have discovered that it is wise to wait to be asked one's opinion rather than constantly volunteering advice. One mom put it this way:

> I believe that my relationship with my adult kids has persevered because I've kept an open line of communication with them. Since they grew up in our home, they already know what I think. They know my thoughts from God's Word and so I don't have to always bring these truths before them. The time for commanding and intense instruction has ended. I want my speech to be winsome, seasoned with the Word, knowing that God will accomplish what he has purposed. This perspective enables me to have peace and trust the Lord to accomplish his purposes in their lives.

A dad agrees that "when the door opens, jump in! In all other cases keep your mouth closed on correction and reproof and open on praise and expressions of love."

In addition, a parent can show respect to an adult child by seeking his advice, especially in matters in which he has expertise (for example anything related to technology).

### Humility Makes the Effort to Communicate

Joan arrives home with the groceries while her son Peter, who is home from college, is sitting in the living room using his laptop. Joan hopes that Peter will spontaneously stop what he is doing and offer to help her. She brings in the first load, rustling the shopping bags so that he will notice, but Peter doesn't even look up from his computer. With each trip from the car Joan becomes angrier, until finally, after she has finished the job, she charges into the living room and chews Peter out for being such a self-centered, thoughtless son. Peter, who feels he was just minding his own business, lashes back and things get ugly.

How could this scene have been avoided? To begin with, Joan could have made it clear that Peter is expected to notice when his mother needs help and pitch in. Or even better, she could have told Peter when she left that she would need help when she returned or, better still, she could have asked for help when she got home. Most likely, Peter would have happily helped if Joan had asked him. Joan was wrong to expect Peter to read her mind, and she was even more at fault for becoming sinfully angry. Joan needed to remember how her Savior never expected her to figure things out on her own, but rather came in humility to reveal the Father's will, often reminding her repeatedly of his commands.

We have already identified several key biblical principles that define minimum expectations parents should have for their adult kids living at home. But beyond these we need to recognize that they have grown up and have both the responsibility and privilege of making their own decisions. While it's true that we may suffer inwardly when we observe how they spend their free time or ache when we see them make unwise choices with friendships or money, we cannot and should not prevent their painful failures. Indeed, they may need to learn through experiencing the consequences of their actions. Part of our letting them go is to inwardly acknowledge that they are accountable to God (not us) for their actions, while we resist the temptation to pressure them to change.

## Humility Respects Their Individuality

One of the most enlightening times in life comes after the birth of your second child. Just when we thought we finally had babies and toddlers figured out, along came our second child who obliterated everything we thought we knew. My wife and I could see differences in our children only days and weeks into their lives. Now that they are adults, their individuality is all the more apparent. One son may flourish by joining the military straight out of high school. Another may go to college and take several years to figure out his direction in life. A third may be an entrepreneur and be on his third business by the time he is twenty-five. Like all parents, we had to learn that each of our sons is an individual. They were not clones of us or of one another.

Humble respect for our kids' individuality flows out of the truth that each one, though different, is created in the image of God. Perhaps one child images God in his love of beauty and desire to create; perhaps another images him in his love of order. We will begin to delight in the differences we see in our children when we begin to see how magnificent and multifaceted our God is. How could he possibly create just one sort of person in his image when his image is so complex?

It is because our children image God in their distinct individuality that we should not attempt to impose our dreams or desires on them. It is wrong for us to tell the artsy son who wants to study music, "Every firstborn son in the Jones family for the past nine generations has been an attorney. We expect you to maintain the family tradition." It is equally wrong to tell our daughter that our "one prayer since before you were born was that you would be a missionary's wife." We have to remember that God has created them as it pleased him, granting that they should reflect his image in their own way. He has decided what callings and gifts to place in their lives. It is not our choice because it is not our life. They need to choose the direction they want to go and the route by which they will get there. If we are supporting our children, we have the right to expect them to be making some sort of progress, but we don't have authority to force them to live out our dreams.

## Humility Admits Sin and Wrong

Relationships can only survive where there is grace. Not only do our children need grace from us, but we also need grace from them. We will never be perfect parents. We will make sinful mistakes, mostly with our words. Rather than standing on our self- righteousness or fearing that we will lose their respect if we admit when we're wrong, we should be quick to humbly seek forgiveness and reconciliation (Matt. 5:23–24). We should freely admit our own struggles, both past and present. Like our kids, we cannot stand on our own righteousness. Our only hope is in Christ and his perfections that have been imputed to us. Because we have the perfect record of the Son of God, we don't have to pretend to be sinless anymore. We can be open, transparent, and vulnerable because we've got a Savior who sees us as we really are and yet loves us.

Tom was upset when his son Dave said, "You are a terrible father. You have never supported or encouraged me in anything I have ever done!" Tom's initial response was to go into "lawyer mode" and defend himself by listing every baseball game and concert he had ever attended and every dollar he had spent to educate and otherwise help Dave. But this approach only served to build higher walls between Tom and his son. The counselor suggested that Tom follow Proverbs 15:1, "A gentle answer turns away wrath" (NASB), and instead say, "Dave, obviously you believe that I have let you down as a father. I want to understand how it is that I have hurt you and how I could be more supportive of you. I am willing to hear whatever you have to say. All I ask is that you try to help me to be a better father."

I personally experienced a transformation in my relationship with one of my sons with whom I was having a sharp conflict. From his standpoint I had controlled his life for nineteen years, and he was very angry. He had declared his independence, and I realized that I could no longer control him by force. I sought to take a genuine interest in understanding exactly how he felt and what he believed. I also allowed him to ask me any question he wanted. I willingly admitted my own struggles and sins. We shed some tears together. While this was very hard, I am convinced that it was the beginning of a fruitful adult-to-adult friendship between my son and me.

It's very difficult to remember that each of us was once an immature young adult. It's also hard to admit that in spite of our advanced years and experience we still sin! God embraces us solely because of his great grace. It is this grace that we should seek to reflect to our adult children. Just as God does not treat us as our sins deserve (Ps. 103:10), we need to incorporate grace into our parenting. Nothing must ever stop us from loving our children.

God's grace helps us assume the best about our kids. "Love . . . hopes all things" (1 Cor. 13:7). Because he has been so gracious with us we can be gracious with them, assume the best, and avoid the temptation to presuppose bad motives, especially in the midst of conflict. Thoughts like, "She did that just to annoy me," "He deliberately slammed the door when he came in late last night," or "He is late because he is goofing off with his worthless friends," can be avoided when we make gracious judgments. Instead of assuming the worst, we should seek the most charitable possible interpretation to the actions and words of others. "She probably was short with me because she was very busy and her mind was on something else," "I am sure that he forgot that there were people sleeping when he made so much noise when he came in," and "Perhaps he had to work overtime tonight" are gracious thoughts that will lead to peace and understanding.

## Humility Overlooks and Forgives

Some of us don't know how good we have it. With kids who are on the honor roll, we complain because they made a B last semester. Or we may regard our child's interest in visiting another church as an act of rebellion, instead of being thankful for their interest in spiritual things. We're tempted to get angry over lights being left on or a dirty cup that didn't make it to the dishwasher. Instead we should rejoice that the Lord does not deal with us in that way. If we're tempted to go nuclear over small problems we need to remember that "a man's discretion makes him slow to anger, and it is his glory to overlook a transgression" (Prov. 19:11, NASB), and "love covers a multitude of sins" (1 Peter 4:8, NASB).

On the other hand, some of us have been deeply wounded by our children. They have squandered our resources, violated our rules, brought shame to our family, and broken our hearts. Sometimes, like the Prodigal Son, they come to their senses and return to the Lord and to us (Luke 15:11–32). It is then that we get the joy of being like the welcoming father who embraced his wayward son and reinstated him in his home. We can forgive them as God, in Christ, has forgiven us (Eph. 4:32). Because Jesus has paid the infinite debt we owed for our sin (Matt. 18:21–35), we can forgive those who have wronged us.

But what if they haven't returned? What if they're still in that far land, squandering their inheritance in wild living and rebellion? While it may be both unwise and wrong to help a wayward child, there is nothing in the Bible that would teach us to be embittered against him or shun him. We can still seek to have a good relationship with him all the while trying to find ways to express our love without enabling sinful behavior. Our attitude should be forgiving like that welcoming father, looking down the road in the hope that one day our dear child will return home so that we can openly forgive and embrace him.

Even though they're adults, they still care what you think and long for your approval. Young men, even those who act like they couldn't care less, strongly feel the need to prove themselves to their fathers. We have also heard from young women who feel the same way about their mothers, wondering if they will ever measure up as a wife and mom in their mothers' eyes. [2]

It's so easy for us to think, "But there is so much that is wrong and immature in the life of my child!" While that may be true, it is both loving and biblical to encourage fellow sinners where you can. In fact, the apostle Paul typically begins his epistles by commending the churches (even the church in Corinth!) before he gets around to admonishing them for their shortcomings. Jesus follows the same practice in his letters to the churches mentioned in Revelation.

I confess that I am a glass-half-empty guy, who tends to be very quick to notice the shortcomings of others, while taking it for granted when they meet expectations. I need to be constantly on the lookout for commendable actions and character traits in my kids. Even unbelieving children were made in God's image and do some things that are commendable (i.e., their vocation, academics, sports, music, etc.). There is much in our children for which we can give thanks to God, while also letting our kids know how thankful we are for them.

Instead of looking for the ways in which our kids fail, we need to become grace detectives. We need to look for evidences (even faint glimmers) of God's grace in their lives and be quick to point them out to ourselves and to them. When we learn the practice of looking for and talking about God's good work in our kids' lives, we'll grow in faith that they can change, and they'll do the same thing. So many times our kids just don't believe that God can or will work in them. Let's help them see how great and powerful he is by pointing out instances of his gracious work every time we think we see it!

## Enjoy Each Other

As I have been observing families over the past three decades, there is one quality that seems to be common in the closest and most successful families. They have fun together! Even if there are disagreements and disappointments, they love each other deeply and enjoy being together. Parenting isn't just about molding your child through discipline. The Lord wants us to enjoy our families. Adult children can be a lot of fun. Play games. Go on outings and family vacations together. Celebrate holidays together. Laugh together. I have been surprised by how much my adult sons still want to spend time with us—playing board games, going to concerts, or just talking. Sometimes I am so busy with all of my duties that I fail to appreciate and enjoy my kids as much as I should.

## Surprise Them with Kindness

While we have emphasized that it is wrong to enable sinful and irresponsible behavior, this does not mean that you cannot do nice things for your kids, even the wayward ones. God does not deal with us according to strict justice (Ps. 103:10; Ezra 9:13), but rather has given us blessing upon blessing. Show grace to your kids. Take them out for meals. Bring them on family trips. Buy them gifts. Show forth the love God has for you in Christ.

Although much of the difficulty that our adult kids have with us flows out of our own sinful hearts, and although none of us is truly as humble, respectful, or encouraging as we should be, the wonderful truth is that the responsibility for a good relationship with our children doesn't rest solely on our shoulders. We are to seek to put on humility, clear communication, forgiveness, and patience. We are also to put off anger, demandingness, and disrespect. But, even so, we are not able to change our own hearts or the hearts of our children. This is the work of the Holy Spirit. It is his job to "turn the hearts of the fathers to the children, and the disobedient to the wisdom of the just" (Luke 1:17) as he works through our words, his Word, and the words of his servants. Only the Spirit can make us truly humble and gentle; it is only by his work that we will learn to be "quick to listen, slow to speak" (James 1:19, NIV). It is only as he infuses the life of Christ into us that we will be willing to become like him: lowly, meek, and gentle. And it is only by the Spirit's power that our children will change and grow into men and women who live lives to the glory of his grace. Let us encourage you today, right now, to put all your trust in him. Pray that he would transform you and your children. Ask that he would grant you the grace to live at peace with them and then throw your entire burden upon him. Why? Because he cares for you.

### Let's Talk More about It

. . . . . . . . . . . . . . . . . . . . . . . . .

1. How would you grade yourself in these areas? Are you slow to speak, eager to listen, and always willing to believe the best?

2. Would you say that you are guilty of nagging? Have you made your expectations of your adult child clear? Do you assume he should read your mind? Are your expectations the same as what you would have of another adult, or are you still treating him like a child?

3. Do you respect the unique individuality of your son or daughter? Do you recognize that the very uniqueness of your child in some way is a reflection of the multifaceted glory of God? Are you guilty of wanting to create them in your own image?

4. Are you a grace detective? When was the last time you sat down with your child and said something like, "I can see God's work in you because . . ."? If you have never done this or are afraid you can't see anything worthy of praise, ask the Lord to give you eyes to see what he's doing, even if it's just a tiny glimmer of grace. Then encourage your child with mounds and mounds of love.

5. Summarize what you've learned in this chapter in four or five sentences.

# 7

# Should Your Home Become a Halfway House?

LYNNE HAD BEEN a very difficult child throughout high school. She liked to party and would sneak out at night with her friends. She didn't apply herself to her schoolwork and was caught cutting class on several occasions. Her parents were relieved when she finally graduated.

A year and a half ago, when Lynne turned eighteen, she moved out of the house to live with her boyfriend. Though the circumstances grieved her folks, they were thankful for the peace and quiet her absence brought. Now they could focus more on their marriage and caring for their younger children.

Yesterday Lynne called to say that she and her boyfriend had broken up and that she would like to move back home because her credit is terrible, and she can't qualify for a place on her own. Although she wants to live at home, Lynne hasn't expressed any remorse for the way she has wronged her parents in the past. When she was asked if she was willing to follow simple house rules she replied with a terse, "Whatever."

As you can imagine, Lynne's parents are bewildered. On one hand it's hard for them to turn away from their child when she needs them. They're concerned about what she might do or where she might have to go if they don't let her come home. But, they're also afraid of the conflict and chaos Lynne will bring with her if they allow her to move home.

## Did We Do Something Wrong?

We all know Christian families whose adult kids have turned away from the Lord and have gotten into trouble with substance abuse, sexual immorality, debt, and crime. Years ago we might have looked at the parents of such kids and wondered, "Where did those parents go wrong?" But now, the Lord has taught us a deeper wisdom born from painful experience—a deeper wisdom that sees that there is more than one reason our kids get into trouble.

Rather than trying to place blame on either our kids, or ourselves, we need to understand that there are a number of factors that determine the kind of adults our kids will become. In our book, *When Good Kids Make Bad Choices*,[1] we identified at least three causes for the outcome of our parenting. First, the Bible teaches that we are responsible to train our children in the discipline and instruction of the Lord. We are to avoid provoking them to anger (Eph. 6:4; Prov. 22:6). Parents who, like Eli, fail to restrain their kids contribute to their children's ruin (Prov. 29:15; 19:18).

Second, our children are responsible for their choices. Think for a moment about the first two children who ever lived, Cain and Abel. What was the difference between them? They were both brought up in the same home under the same influences. Their parents instructed them equally in the ways of the Lord. But they grew up to be very different people. Abel chose to honor the Lord in worship, while Cain turned from God, refusing to heed his direct warning, and killed his brother. That Cain was responsible for his own choices is made plain by God's warning and judgment of Cain and not his parents. Similarly, Ezekiel 18 gives us the record of three generations of men—a righteous father, his unrighteous son, and his righteous grandson. In this example each generation is responsible before the Lord to choose the right way, no matter what his father or son does.

We shouldn't be surprised that one child may choose to embrace the way of the Lord while another rejects it. Jesus understood the conflict that the gospel would bring into our homes when he warned that the truth about his salvation and grace would actually divide families! Mothers and daughters, sons and fathers would be estranged because of it. Some will rebelliously remain alienated in the darkness, while others will walk out into the light with you (Luke 12:51–53). Division is the inevitable result of the truth of the gospel. It will divide us from our natural families and join us to our spiritual family, the church. It may even be that our deepest and most satisfying relationships will not be with those of our biological family, but rather with our brothers, sisters, sons, and daughters in the faith.[2] It also is comforting to know that God himself knows what it is like to have wayward children as he speaks through the prophet Isaiah about his people

Israel: "Sons I have reared and brought up, but they have revolted against Me (Isa. 1:2)."

Finally, the third and most important reason our kids turn out like they do is God's sovereign grace. Our children are born sinners who must be given spiritual life from above (Ps. 51:5; Eph. 2). Even if we were perfect parents, without God's grace they would rebel. Even if they were given to us as completely innocent blank slates, we would ruin them by our own sin. There is no book or seminar that contains a foolproof formula to win our kids to the Lord.[3] God alone can save our kids (John 6:44). The amazing and delightful news is that sometimes he chooses to do so despite our failures and our kids' sinful hearts.

## When Is Your Help Too Much Help?

Adult kids who get into adult-sized trouble with money and the law have a remarkable ability to make their problem ours. "If my car is repossessed and I lose my job," they might threaten, "it will be all your fault because you didn't help me." But is this a true statement? Is it true that it's our responsibility to make their car payments? Although a valid question, it is not the only or most important one. We should also ask whether making that payment is an act of love. While being helpful and generous usually seems like the loving thing to do, we must consider if it always is. As counselors, we have watched parents bail their sons out of jail for DUI or domestic violence. We've seen them pay off their daughters' credit card debts. When our adult children get into adult-sized trouble, we have to ask ourselves whether our help really is helpful or not. Are we really loving them?

When Nate approached his mother, Jan, about paying his overdue car insurance bill, he knew that she wouldn't want him to break the law by driving uninsured. He also knew that it was important to his mother that he be able to get himself to school and work. Making her responsible for his debt seemed logical to Nate. But Jan saw the situation differently. She remembered how Nate had purchased a plasma TV and an Xbox for his bedroom last month. When she remembered how she had to scrimp and save to buy a new purse for herself she was deeply angered that Nate had put her in this situation. But she decided to pay for the insurance anyway because she thought she had no choice. She loved Nate and he needed her help. But was she really helping him?

Chris and Sarah came to see us concerning their thirty-five-year-old son Roger who was deeply in debt largely due to gambling. Roger is also at risk of going to prison for past illegal business dealings, though Roger says that the crimes were his partner's fault. Because they love Roger and because they don't want to see him go to jail, they've been helping him with his legal expenses. In addition, Roger's wife is threatening to divorce him due to his repeated adulterous affairs. Because of the conflict in his home, he often sleeps at his parents' house to avoid his wife. In an effort to help Roger, his dad, Chris, has given him a job in his business. But Roger spends very little productive time in the office. Chris isn't quite sure what Roger is doing with all his time, but he knows that he isn't working.

Roger's incessant trouble and intrusion into the lives (and bank accounts) of his parents are creating growing tensions in their own marriage because they can't agree about how much to help him. Chris and Sarah were both shocked and relieved to learn that it wasn't their job to solve their adult son's problems. In fact, rather than helping him, their well-meant efforts had exacerbated the problem, making Roger more and more dependent and irresponsible. Even though just the opposite seemed true, they had failed to love and respect Roger as an individual created in the image of God and responsible to live maturely before him. We counseled Chris and Sarah to disengage themselves from their unrepentant son's life and let him face the consequences of his own choices.

## What Does Real Love Look Like?

Our young adults can be charming, persuasive, and manipulative—especially when they want our help. They have lived with us long enough to know exactly what we want to hear. "I think the Lord is getting my attention. I am going back to church. This time I am going to really change and serve the Lord." These are words we would all love to hear if they were spoken in sincerity. But before we believe everything they say, especially when they're asking for our help, we should wait to see if there is any measurable repentance, and even if there is, we must ask ourselves whether helping them is loving and wise. Our dollars won't buy their love or repentance, and we can't fund their admission into God's kingdom. Only the Holy Spirit can truly change their hearts.

Sadly, many of our wayward children have an entitlement mentality. They see that we have resources, but because many of them don't work hard themselves, they don't respect the hard work it took for us to acquire them. Their foolish reasoning is, "If you have money and can help me, you should. After all, if I had money and you needed my help, I would give it to you." Because "every man's way is right in his own eyes" (Prov. 21:2, NASB), they fail to see how lazy they've been, or how they may have squandered their own opportunities and resources. All they see is what you have and they truly believe that because you are a loving parent, everything you own should be theirs.

Why do so many of us fail to respond to our children in a way that demonstrates that we really love them? Why do we say yes when no is what they really need to hear? The truth is that many of us are motivated by guilt and fear rather than genuine love for our kids. Thoughts such as, "If I had been a better parent she wouldn't be in this trouble," "I don't care if he is guilty. I can't stand the idea of my baby going to jail," or "If we don't let her come home (even though she refuses to work or respect house rules), she'll be out on the street," plague us and distort our attainment of wisdom. Although we love them and want to reassure them that they can rely on us, the truth is that we often bail out our kids for our own benefit, to spare us from feeling guilty or seeing our kids suffer. In cases like these, we're not doing what is best for our children, we're doing what makes us feel good about ourselves. When we serve ourselves we're not serving the Lord or our kids. Bailing our kids out of trouble all the time isn't an act of love for them—it's self-love.

### How Can We Begin to Really Love Them?

It's obvious that we need real help. In many ways we're self-deceived and confused just like our children. We think we're being loving, but the opposite is true. We know there's something wrong with the way that we're thinking and responding, but we just can't seem to get clarity about what's right. We need real help and wisdom, help that can only come from the Lord.

The wonderful news is that the Lord has made a very precious promise to us in our hour of need. This is what he has promised: "If any of you lacks wisdom, let him ask God, who gives generously to all without reproach, and it will be given him" (James 1:5). Think of that! The Lord God, who is the fount of all wisdom and understanding, has promised to share his wisdom with us if we ask. So ask. Ask that he would open your eyes and grant you the benefit of understanding how to respond in a way that's wise, that will please him, and that will demonstrate real love for him and for your kids.

But once we've prayed for wisdom (and this prayer should never cease), there's one place God's wisdom perfectly resides. Although we can see his wisdom in nature and through those around us, the Bible is the only sufficient source of wisdom for our lives. In faith we need to trust in his Word, rather than merely following our own thoughts and feelings (Prov. 3:5–6). We can wholeheartedly rest in his provision for us in Scripture, because he has promised that he won't allow us to be tempted beyond what we are able (1 Cor. 10:13). He has sworn that he will never leave us nor forsake us (Heb. 13:5).

Although God's wisdom does reside in Scripture, it is also appropriate to seek counsel from others who are wise and who understand the principles in God's word (Prov. 11:14). Because we're so inherently enmeshed in their lives, we often don't think very clearly when it comes to our kids, especially when they are in trouble. We need objective (and sometimes tough) godly advice from friends who are not afraid of wounding us by their counsel when necessary (Prov. 27:6).

Sometimes godly friends can help give you an understanding of the root of your child's waywardness. Even though the world might say that their sinful behavior (drunkenness, gambling, sexual immorality, and laziness) is a disease, thus making them victims, the Bible teaches that they are responsible for the choices they make. Your child's lifestyle reveals what he believes and what he worships (his idols). Perhaps your counselors may even help you see that your child's greatest need is conversion even though he may have made "professions" of faith as a child.

## Many Times Love Means Saying No

If you recognize your own failures as a parent, confess your sin to God, but don't compound your guilt by financing more sin in the life of your child. One young man told us,

"Parents have much leverage in the lives of their adult kids. And when it comes to finances, they should not be afraid to use it. While it might not work, it certainly won't facilitate or fund their rebelliousness." By continuing to fund an errant child's lifestyle, you may be circumventing the very consequences the Lord might use to bring your children to himself. Remember that the Prodigal Son only came to his senses when he was in the far country, alone, hungry, and broke. It would have been unwise and unloving for his father to continue to send him yet more money to squander, thus extending his stay in the land of loose living.

When those who are lazy go without the nice things money can buy, they may be motivated to acquire a skill and work hard (Prov. 19:15; 16:26). Many adult children, because of the unwise interventions of their parents, have not yet made a connection between their waywardness and the troubles that ordinarily ensue. Often they see themselves as unlucky victims who deserve help. One of the hardest things for parents to do is to let their children reap what they have sown (Gal. 6:7). As another young man told us,

> If an adult child will not respect the expectations of his parents while living at home, he has no right to prey upon his parents' hospitality. . . . One of the worst ways a parent can undermine their own respectability in the eyes of their children is to offer up empty threats while continuing to enable their child to live irresponsibly.

## Saying No Isn't Saying I Don't Love You Anymore

Because God never turns away his wayward children who come to him for help (Matt. 11:28–30), we should never turn our backs on our children who come to us, no matter how much they have hurt or shamed us. We are all prodigal sons and daughters who have been gifted with the amazing grace of a heavenly Father who has welcomed us home, in spite of our many sins, and has blessed us immeasurably beyond what we deserve or could have imagined. An unwed pregnant daughter should be welcomed home and encouraged for her choice to keep her child. A son who has been enslaved to substance abuse should be offered love and hope (and drug testing). We need God's grace in Christ as much as they do. Abraham Piper advises, "Plead with them more than you rebuke them. Be gentle in your disappointment. What really concerns you is that your child is destroying herself, not that she's breaking the rules. . . . Her conscience can condemn her by itself."[4]

This does not mean, however, that we help our wayward children unconditionally, repeatedly, and on their terms. The Prodigal Son was broken and repentant when he came home. Other wayward children return home only as a last resort— they see home as the only remaining port in a storm, with no intention of changing their ways. Even in such cases we should offer help, but only in such a way as pleases the Lord.

Your adult child's return home should be seen as an opportunity for you to complete your parenting job of preparing her for adult life. Several parents we surveyed wrote favorably about giving second chances, but strongly opposed repeatedly bailing a child out of the same kinds of problems. As Albert Einstein said, "Insanity is repeating the same thing over and over while expecting different results."[5] Rather than merely bailing your child out of his immediate problem, seek to deal with the root causes (Prov. 4:23; Mark 7:21–23), such as a poor work ethic, a lack of self control, or an unwillingness to defer gratification. Otherwise, you will be called upon to bail him out again and again. If your child merely wants your resources and doesn't want your counsel in dealing with the cause, you probably should give her neither.[6]

## When Your Home Is a Halfway House

An adult child who is living at home because he has gotten into trouble is in a different situation than the child who has remained at home during a normal transition to full independence. Ordinarily, as maturity increases and trust is built, our involvement in our kids' decisions decreases. But the wayward child has failed to mature and in most cases has shattered parental trust. Therefore, the parent may be forced to exercise more control as a condition of the child continuing to live at home.[7]

For example, if your child has moved home because of overwhelming debt it may be necessary to require that she work full-time, live within a budget (with a plan to pay off the debt), and be accountable for what she does with her money. Or, if your son has had problems with substance abuse, you may require that he take periodic drug tests and be fully accountable for how he spends his time and money. You may also choose to require that your child receive biblical counseling to address the heart causes of his problems.

But what if your child objects to these requirements as a violation of a more typical adult status? While it is true that we are not treating our kids in the same way that we would other adults, that's simply because they have made choices that have necessitated this change in relationship. Of course, because they are adults, they can always choose to live on their own. But if they choose to live at home, they can't expect to have it both ways—they can't expect to have all the privileges of adulthood without any of the consequences for the choices they've made as adults. In cases like these, we're serving the function of a halfway house, helping our kids to get their lives back on track, offering help, and expecting a responsive willingness to receive it. Of course, this transition in our relationship with them will be hard on both of us. They'll feel humiliated and angry. They'll be tempted to be deceptive. We'll be tempted to impatience, overcontrol, and humiliation too. Only with the Lord's help will we be able to be as strong and as patient as needed.

When a young adult has to return home, the usual trust between a parent and child has been shattered. Wayward adult children often lie in order to avoid consequences or to get what they want from others. Honesty should be a nonnegotiable condition of turning your home into a halfway house. If a pattern of dishonesty continues, the privilege of living at home must be forfeited.[8]

## When the Privilege of Your Home Should Be Forfeited

In the Old Testament, as part of the law that Moses gave to the nation of Israel, a provision was made for wayward adult children who refused to change. These sad and terrifying words were written for the good of the nation and families who faced the misery of having a "stubborn and rebellious son who will not obey the voice of his father or his mother . . . [who] is a glutton and a drunkard." The parents would take the child to the elders of his city and if the elders agreed with the parents' perspective, "all the men of the city shall stone him to death with stones" (Deut. 21:18–21).

While we recognize that under the new covenant wayward children are no longer punished in this way, we can learn important principles from this text that apply to us today. First, it's obvious that this text is referring to wayward adults,

112

not kids—wayward toddlers generally can't be described as gluttons and drunkards! Second, we learn that the Bible acknowledges that there is such a thing as an incorrigible child—a person who is completely out of control and beyond correction. We also learn that the Lord holds the wayward young adult, not his parents, responsible for his choices, as it is the child who is punished. Third, we learn that we need to be concerned about the effect that a wayward child will have upon others because the reason God gives for punishing the child is to "purge the evil from your midst." A rebellious young adult can turn a home into a war zone and often seeks to influence or even harm other siblings. Finally, we see that some cases of rebellion are so severe that drastic measures are necessary.

What kind of drastic measures are appropriate under the new covenant? If your child is a member of the church, the church leaders should be involved, and if he refuses to repent, church discipline will need to be exercised (Matt. 18:15–20; 1 Cor. 5). If your child is breaking the law, instead of hiring lawyers to help her avoid the consequences of what she has done, you should allow her to experience the result of her actions (Rom. 13:1–7; Gal. 6:7; 1 Peter 2:14). Perhaps it will even be necessary for a parent to turn a child over to the authorities for crimes he has committed (i.e., theft, dealing drugs, illegal possession of weapons, murder, etc.). Here's the bottom line: when our children are not willing to live in our home and abide by the rules we've set, they should not be allowed to remain in our home. Remember that his lack of a place to stay is the result of his folly and is not your fault. If a child refuses to leave, you may even need to change the locks or get a restraining order.

Putting a child out of the house does not mean, however, that we must totally shun him. We can still invite him over for meals or to participate in family events. No matter what your child does (whether your daughter has an abortion or your son declares himself to be a homosexual) you should still love him (and tell him so), just as God loves you in spite of your sin. And then, whenever your child is truly repentant and has demonstrated the fruit of repentance by changing his lifestyle, you can allow him to come back home.

### Loving Our Lost Children

Our love for our children is not conditioned upon their being converted. Nor should we refuse to offer help to an unbelieving child. We should grasp the opportunity to live the gospel before our unsaved children by showing them grace and forgiveness. Just as God shows common grace to the lost by allowing them to live in and enjoy his wonderful creation (Matt. 5:45), we too can offer our lost children the benefits of being in our home. While our greatest desire for them is their conversion, we can also give them an opportunity to get their lives in order, learn a trade, reduce their debt, or win freedom from substance abuse. The wonderful truth is that, because we never stop being their parent, we can continue to encourage, love, and challenge them.

## Let's Talk More about It
. . . . . . . . . . . . . . . . . . . . . .

1. What follows is a quote from Abraham Piper written to parents of wayward kids: "Point them to Christ. Your rebellious child's real problem is not drugs or sex or cigarettes or pornography or laziness or crime or cussing

or slovenliness or homosexuality or being in a punk rock band. The real problem is that they don't see Jesus clearly. The best thing you can do for them . . . is to show them Christ. It is not a simple or immediate process, but the sins in their life that distress you and destroy them will only begin to fade away when they see Jesus more like he actually is. . . . The only ultimate reason to pray for them, welcome them, plead with them, email them, eat with them, or take an interest in their interests is so that their eyes will be opened to Christ. And not only is he the only point—he's the only hope. When they see the wonder of Jesus, satisfaction will be redefined. He will replace the pathetic vanity of the money, or the praise of man, or the high, or the orgasm that they are staking their eternities on right now. Only his grace can draw them from their perilous pursuits and bind them safely to himself—captive, but satisfied."[9] How does the above speak to your heart? In light of this what changes should you make in the way you relate to your adult kids?

2. Stop now and pray that the Lord would open the eyes of your child and make himself beautiful to him. You can exemplify that beauty as you continue to love and welcome your dear child—even if you've had to ask him to stop living with you.

3. Be encouraged that your labor is not in vain, as one formerly wayward son wrote, "When I was not a Christian yet and living a very worldly life, I couldn't get my parents' voice out of my head instructing me in the Lord's ways. Their words would convict me. I guess that God was talking to me through their words and it showed me that my parents loved me." Do you believe that the Lord is continuing to speak to your child?

4. Spend time in prayer that the Lord would encourage your heart and enable you to continue on in this fight remembering to "be steadfast, immovable, always abounding in the work of the Lord, knowing that in the Lord your labor is not in vain" (1 Cor. 15:58).

5. Summarize what you've learned in this chapter in four or five sentences.

# 8

# Wisely Navigating the Money Maze

THE JONESES had always been financially blessed. Bill Jones enjoyed a successful career and was generous with his wife, Nancy, and their three children. Every Christmas there was a mountain of gifts around the tree, and every year Bill made sure that their children's hopes and dreams were surpassed with the best toys, video games, cell phones, and iPods available. When his kids finished high school, Bill paid for the finest private universities and made sure that they had whatever they wanted in terms of cars, clothes, and computers. But Bill is grieved that after spending all of this money he doesn't feel close to his kids. Furthermore, even though they have completed college, they are constantly asking him for money, such that he feels like a human ATM. He wonders where he went wrong. Why don't his children appreciate him?

Timothy's spiritual father, Paul, warned his dear son that "the love of money is a root of all kinds of evils. It is through this craving that some have wandered away from the faith and pierced themselves with many pangs" (1 Tim. 6:10). The love of money is deadly to our spiritual lives because money brings with it the deception of self-sufficiency and independence. It makes us feel strong, able to acquire the desires of our hearts; it fools us into thinking we're invincible, able to protect ourselves from difficulties or discomforts. It teaches us to disdain trust in God. Money is so dangerous that Jesus warns either he will be our God or money will—there's no middle ground here. We cannot serve both God and money (Matt. 6:24).

Our children have grown up in a materialistic culture that continually tells them that acquiring money is the purpose of life. They are incessantly bombarded by commercials touting the latest gadget or shiny, new car. They're told a lie: "If you could just obtain *this* (whatever the *this* du jour might be), you'll be happy, people will like you, and you'll find acceptance and friends. Life will be fun! You don't need to wait to have this . . . just charge it and you'll be so happy you did!" These are the lies they've heard their entire lives, and unless they consciously choose daily to love God more than money, they'll fall prey to all the sorrow and pangs the love of this god brings with him.

The love of money is the root of all sorts of evils, so it's no wonder that this is one area where conflicts abound. Conflicts abound here because our relationship to money is a watershed issue—it's a litmus test of our worship. If we love money, it will cause conflicts with our kids. This is one of those places where we're very vulnerable and where sin overflows. In light of the intrinsic danger of misusing money, worshiping it, or using it to manipulate others, all of us desperately need wisdom from above.

Every time we ignore the wisdom of the Lord and substitute our own homemade purposes and strategies, we are setting ourselves up for evil, piercing, and pangs. Again, handling money in a godly way is very difficult, and we must deliberately attend to God's wisdom in order to avoid these sorrows. For instance, when parents ignore the wisdom of Proverbs 17:18 that says, "One who lacks sense gives a pledge and puts up security in the presence of his neighbor," and unwisely cosign on their children's debts, they shouldn't be surprised at the pain they feel when they're left holding the (empty) bag.

## The Wisdom of the Lord and Our Money

In October of 2009, the American public debt was a whopping $11,907,608,545,823.24.[1] In addition to our public debt, at the end of 2008, Americans' personal credit card debt reached $972.73 billion, up 1.12 percent from 2007.[2] That's around $9,000 for every adult in America. In light of these staggering statistics, it should be obvious to each of us that there is a real need to warn our adult children (and each other) against debt. Why? Because as Proverbs 22:7 says, "The borrower becomes the lender's slave" (NASB). When our young people do not understand and embrace the Lord's wisdom regarding their money, they lose their freedom to give generously and make decisions based on personal goals and godly desires. Young people may fall into sexual temptation and sin because they are in debt and cannot afford to get married. They are enslaved to the lender and must spend their money trying to pay off their loans, which is especially difficult given the high interest rates that credit card companies usually charge.

119

Rather than encouraging them to impulsively acquire everything they think they want, we need to teach them to postpone gratification and to save up for major purchases (Prov. 6:8; 13:11). We need to help them see the value of making a budget and of sticking to it. Why? Because as Proverbs 21:5 warns us, "The plans of the diligent lead surely to advantage, but everyone who is hasty comes surely to poverty" (NASB). We need to help them learn to promptly pay their financial obligations (Prov. 3:27–28) and remind them of the blessedness of being generous to the Lord's work and to those in need (Prov. 3:9–10; 11:25).

One of the reasons our kids get into financial trouble is because they've not acquired a skill that will produce much wealth. Because both a minimum wage worker and one who works a skilled position put in time and effort, getting trained with a marketable skill is obviously preferable. Our sons need to be taught to gain a marketable skill and a work ethic so that they can provide for a family (Prov. 10:4; 22:29). Our daughters too need to be trained to work hard like the woman in Proverbs 31. Because we cannot be certain when or if our daughters will be married, it is wise for them to also acquire skills by which they could take care of themselves if the need should arise.

Hard work builds both character and a sense of responsibility. Young adults should be warned against trying to circumvent God's design for acquiring wealth through get-rich-quick schemes like gambling. It is estimated that in 2006 Americans spent *nine hundred and ten billion* dollars gambling—that's more than was earned by Exxon-Mobil, Wal-Mart, General Motors, Chevron, and Ford combined. [3] Again Proverbs puts it so clearly, "He who tills his land will have plenty of bread, but he who pursues worthless things lacks sense" (Prov. 12:11, NASB). Greed, superstition, and laziness fund the gambling industry in America and our young people need to be seriously warned about trying to get money without earning it through labor.

Our children also need to be taught that because we live in a fallen world work is often hard. The curse that was initiated after the fall in the garden of Eden is still in effect, even though for those of us who are believers much of the sting has been removed from it. But the truth remains that we still live with computers that crash and weeds that grow in our carefully tended gardens. Neither our children nor we can always pursue our dream career in the jobs we love. Sometimes we have to work hard just to make ends meet.

### Neither a Borrower, Nor a Lender, Nor a Cosigner Be

We've seen how the Bible warns us against borrowing money, but lending money can be equally dangerous. Although we may be attempting to help our kids by loaning them money, we may actually end up harming our relationships. This happens particularly when they're not making much of an effort to pay us back, and we see that they've got a new gadget or are spending money on expensive vacations. Ironically, it is often the borrower who is most embittered against the lender. I used to wonder why anyone would resent a family member who was kind enough to lend to him in a time of need. Then I remembered the truth from Proverbs 22:7, that the borrower becomes the lender's slave. No one likes to feel like a slave, so the borrower may resent and even avoid those who have lent him money, because he feels guilty and inferior.

But, if you do choose to lend money to a child, it is important that the terms be made very clear and are put in writing. If the amount is significant, it may be appropriate to include a note with your will or trust that this child's debt is to be repaid to the estate out of his inheritance.

We would even more strongly urge you to never cosign for your kids (or anyone else for that matter). Again, Proverbs strongly warns us against this practice,

> Be not one of those who give pledges,
>> who put up security for debts.
> If you have nothing with which to pay,
>> why should your bed be taken from under you?
>> (Prov. 22:26–27)

If our kids can't get credit on their own, it's probably because the bank has concluded that the risk of nonpayment is significant. What this means is that they really can't afford whatever it is they are hoping to buy and probably shouldn't get it. If you choose to cosign, the bank will come after you if they fail to repay it, and you may find yourself with a financial problem or a ruined credit rating.

If you're convinced that there is a legitimate need for the money, and you can afford to, then give it to them. Don't lend it. But, if after all this, you still choose to give a loan or cosign on one, please be prepared to lose the entire amount without rancor or bitterness. If you can afford to lose the entire amount, then you can always give a loan that will be forgiven once your child has demonstrated maturity by paying it off in part.

## Wisdom in Leaving an Inheritance

Last week I spent the afternoon with an older friend just to listen to his stories about his children and his grandchildren. One thing that impressed me was how much my friend and his wife had given financially to help his kids, three of whom he helped with the down payments on their homes. They also had been generous with their grandchildren, giving significant help to fund their education. Although it might seem otherwise, my friend is not a rich man; he let it slip that he had recently been forced to sell some of his coin collection to pay for his own dental work.

As I pondered his generosity I was reminded of how much parents and grandparents have sacrificially invested in future generations of their family members, and how much my wife and I have been blessed through our parents and grandparents. A 2007 survey found that nine out of ten parents give money to their grown kids for major expenses such as credit card balances, car insurance, and student loans.[4] In the previous chapter we warned against using our financial resources to enable irresponsibility, but in this chapter, we'll encourage you to see some of the positive ways parents should consider offering financial help to their grown kids. As Proverbs says, "A good man leaves an inheritance to his children's children. . . . House and wealth are an inheritance from fathers" (Prov. 13:22; 19:14; also see 2 Cor. 12:14).

Although it is typical to bequeath resources to the next generation upon our death, many parents choose to invest in their kids beforehand, rather than making their kids wait to inherit, by which time the kids may be middle-aged themselves and not need the money. In the agrarian economy of biblical times the inheritance would usually be land the son could use as a means to produce income for his family. In our culture, most people increase their earning power through education by acquiring marketable skills (Prov. 22:29). Therefore, it is good that many parents help their children acquire the means to make a livelihood by helping to pay for their college education.[5] Of course, not everyone should go to college. Parents can also help their young adults learn a trade through an apprenticeship or vocational training, or they can help their entrepreneurial kids start their first business.

Parents who desire to do so may find many other ways to bless their grown children financially, such as assisting them with the down payment on a house. Others have brought the extended family together by providing special vacations and family events that would have been beyond the means of their children and their spouses. Many have set up a college fund for their grandchildren (Prov. 13:22). And most of us have rendered aid in the case of an emergency, when their adult children have experienced a financial crisis such as job loss or medical bills.

While the book of Proverbs generally commends leaving our children an inheritance, it also warns us that, "an inheritance gained hastily in the beginning will not be blessed in the end" (Prov. 20:21). Sadly, many young people have shown themselves to be incapable of handling their inheritance wisely. If that's the case with your kids, we would encourage you to designate a trustee to help even grown children manage their estate, and to limit their access to their inheritance until they reach a particular age.

### When to Say Yes, When to Say No

When our kids come to us for financial help, we should take time to really hear them out. We show love and respect by carefully listening to them and to their reasons for needing the money now. Perhaps they'll acknowledge past failures or have a plan to repay the money, and we need to hear that from them before we make a decision. To insure that we're not funding an ungodly lifestyle, we need to ask probing questions that will help us discern whether this is a godly plan or just another way to get what they want without waiting for it. Perhaps it would be better for our kids to postpone gratification of this desire or to save for it over time. If our kids have squandered their money on luxury items, such as the latest cell phone and computer, it's probably best to say no. And because we're going to try to be wise and analyze this decision biblically, it's best to tell them that we will pray about this decision and wait a day or two before letting them know our answer. That way our kids will begin to understand that we can't be pressured into giving them money and that it's inappropriate to treat us as veritable ATM machines.

If after prayer and consideration we're still not sure that we should give them what they ask, we can always make a counterproposal like, "I will match you dollar for dollar for what you save for a car (up to five thousand dollars) over the next six months." Even if we come to the conclusion that we must say no, we can always do so gently, with respect and love, keeping in mind how we feel when we are disappointed in a request we've made.

Most importantly, we've got to guard against being manipulated by fear of the consequences if we don't help them. If they are angry with us, threaten to cut off relationship, or tell us of terrible consequences if we don't bail them out (again), it is most loving for us to stand our ground and help them experience the natural results of what may have been irresponsible behavior. We are responsible to love them and care for them, but only as appropriate. We are not responsible to make every wrong decision they've made right nor enable them to avoid the pain that their wrong decisions have caused. The pain in the stomach of the Prodigal Son taught him lessons his heart refused to learn. One mom wrote,

We had an instance in which we almost bailed our son out of financial trouble. Though he wasn't living in our home, we knew what was going on because he was getting calls at our home number. He hadn't been making payments on his student loan, so the loan was turned over to a collection agency. The agency offered to settle for a lesser amount if he could come up with the amount in full. We considered putting his debt on our credit card. It would have saved him a lot of grief (and a lot of money in late charges, not to mention his credit rating) if we had assumed the debt and allowed him to make payments to us. And yet, we knew that wasn't the right thing to do. We decided we wouldn't bail him out because we realized our son needed to understand the consequences of not making timely payments. Besides, if he was irresponsible in paying the original lender, why would we think he would be any different with us? It wasn't easy to do, but we needed to exercise wise judgment. Thankfully, he understood our position, and it didn't come between us.

Many parents, hoping that their children have learned their lesson and are repentant, choose to help them out of financial trouble by paying off their debts.[6] Because God has showered such mercy on us, we can't say that it's always wrong to help. For the sake of the gospel, it may be good to err once (or even twice) on the side of grace. A mother writes, "Financial help should be given to our adult children when we know that they are putting forth the effort to be financially responsible but are having difficulty. We should team up with them to get through the challenges whether that be allowing them to come home for a season or giving them money."

## Saying Yes to Your Spouse and No to Your Child

The primary relationship that parents have is with each other, not with their children, no matter how it may seem.

Because the Bible teaches that children should and will eventually leave us, the relationship we have with one another is more lasting and important. And even though we know that this relationship is the one we must concentrate on, we also admit that it's fraught with difficulties. Let's admit it, there are plenty of things to disagree about when it's just the two of us. But if we throw in the dynamic of a persuasive, manipulative child, the possibilities for conflict multiply exponentially. Frequently one parent wants to help while the other thinks that helping this time is wrong. We've seen one parent ruin the financial stability of the entire family by throwing money at a wayward child in defiance of the other spouse's wishes. Because we believe that one reason God has established marriage is for the strength and protection of both partners, we recommend that no financial help be offered without both parents being in agreement. Then, if they cannot achieve unity on their own, they should seek godly counsel to mediate (Phil. 4:2–3).

## The Wisdom of Saying Yes to One and No to Another

When we consider what kind of help we'll give to our kids, we've first got to realize that it will be virtually impossible to treat each one with perfect equality. Because of their unique gifting and interests, perhaps one will receive more money than others. For instance, a child that is very gifted musically will likely take more money to support than a child who just likes to ride his skateboard. Some kids need more help with medical, dental, and orthodontic bills than their siblings. Because you bought that piano for one doesn't mean that you owe an equal amount to his brother.

Also, because your children and their circumstances are different, it may not be best to treat them with absolute equality. The friend whom I mentioned earlier gave significant help to three of his kids when they bought their first homes, but did not need to help a fourth. You may have a child who goes to seminary and then becomes a missionary, to whom you will give significant support as an investment in the kingdom of God. His brother who is a lawyer and his sister who works as a pediatrician shouldn't (and probably won't) expect the same treatment. Similarly, if one daughter-in-law needs expensive surgery, which her insurance does not adequately cover, you may choose to give out of love for her. This does not mean that your other daughters-in-law should receive the same amount of money. Finally, if you have a wayward child whom you suspect would misuse an inheritance to his own detriment, you might be wise to keep him from it or at least to put his share under the stewardship of a trustee. One mother we know chose to treat each of her children equally, even though her son Peter had been addicted to drugs for over twenty years. When she died, Peter, along with his two sisters, each inherited about fifty thousand dollars. Within a year Peter had squandered the money, mostly on drugs, and was in worse shape than ever.

Having said all that, there are few matters over which families have fought more than money. This problem is not new to our age. Jesus was asked by a man to force his brother to share the inheritance (Luke 12:13), and Joseph's brothers hated him because of their father's favoritism. Our children may become embittered if they sense that we prefer one above the other. If, however, we choose to help one child more than the others, or if we treat them differently in our will, we should explain our choices and reasons with them so that there will be real communication and relationships won't be broken.

## What Should We Require from Them?

Godly parents have differing opinions as to whether their grown kids living at home should be forced to pay rent or some share of household expenses. There is no universal right or wrong answer to this question, but several factors may determine a wise course of action.

The first is whether the parents need the money. Some parents are struggling to make it financially so it is only right that their working adult child, who is eating the food, using the utilities, etc., pay a fair share of household expenses. On the other hand, some parents don't want or need money from their adult kids and are happy to let them save for their future while living at home.

Another factor is whether the young adult is acting wisely with his finances. Some parents teach their children responsibility by making them pay rent. One mom writes,

> One of the best things I did was collect rent from my children when they had graduated from college and had a job. . . . They were working but not sure of where they wanted to settle. They stayed home an average of one year to eighteen months. When they paid the rent, it went into a savings account for them. They got it when they left to be on their own—a total surprise to them, and a nice nest egg.

If we decide to help our kids out financially, we must be very careful to avoid using money to control and manipulate them. As adults they have the right to make their own decisions and we should never use money as a way to claim some right over them or to insist that they do things our way. The ideal way for parents to help their kids financially is to say, "We love you and want to help out a little bit. We trust that you will use this money wisely." Many young (and not so young) couples have been tremendously blessed by financial help from their parents. On the other hand, if money is being given for a particular purpose (e.g., education) or to help your child out of trouble (e.g., paying off a debt), then it is proper to expect the money to be used as agreed and appropriate to seek accountability.

129

## *The Greatest Inheritance of All*

We're sure that you understand that the most important inheritance you can offer your children is spiritual (Eph. 1:11; Heb. 9:15). The American founding father Patrick Henry wrote the following in his will:

> I have now disposed of all my property to my family: there is one thing more I wish I could give them, and that is, the Christian religion. If they had that and I had not given them one shilling, they would be rich; and if they had not that, and I had given them all the world, they would be poor.[7]

As this chapter draws to a close, let us remind you of one of our favorite verses about wealth—and it's not from Proverbs! "For you know the grace of our Lord Jesus Christ, that though he was rich, yet for your sake he became poor, so that you by his poverty might become rich" (2 Cor. 8:9). Because of our foolishness we have all, parents and children alike, owed an infinite debt to a righteous, loving Father. In spite of the great danger to himself in doing so, Jesus became surety (a cosigner) for our debt and paid it in full on our behalf. He bore all the wrath that was meant to be ours and then he transferred his immense wealth to our empty accounts. He has enriched us spiritually beyond all human measure. In light of the wonderful gift we've been given in Christ, we should continue to strive to be generous with our children and to wisely share all that we have that is good with them.

### Let's Talk More about It
· · · · · · · · · · · · · · · · · · · · · · · ·

1. Is the love of money that Paul talked about a problem in your heart? Is it a problem in your family? In what ways has it been the root of all sorts of evils?

2. Has there been conflict with your spouse over your use of finances with your adult kids? If you're unable to resolve this issue on your own, are you willing to go to your pastor or a biblical counselor for help?

3. If you have loaned money to a child or cosigned on a loan, perhaps you should decide in your heart to let that money go as a gift to them, mirroring the Lord's gift to you. After spending time in prayer and in counsel with your spouse and others, and if your child is being responsible in repaying the debt, why not let them know that you've decided it was wrong for you to get involved in this way and that you've had a change of heart about how it will be repaid? Remember that the slave and the borrower have much in common.

4. Do you have a clear will or a living trust? With the development of sites such as *www.legalzoom.com*, arranging your affairs beforehand is easy and inexpensive. Be sure to communicate your plans to your kids and go over the papers with them before a difficult situation arises.

5. Summarize what you've learned in this chapter in four or five sentences.

# 9

# Marriage: Our Dreams, Their Dreams

TWENTY-SIX-YEAR-OLD CAROL HAD always been "daddy's girl." She and her father Glen shared the same forthright personality and held the same religious and political beliefs. When Carol was away at school she met a fine Christian military officer named Paul who approached Glen to ask permission to court Carol. Glen gladly gave his approval. As the courtship progressed, however, Glen objected strongly to some of Paul's doctrinal beliefs, the most offensive being his belief in predestination. Glen was even more disturbed to learn that his daughter Carol had embraced Paul's theology and was attending church with him. Glen decided enough was enough. He forbade Paul to ever see Carol again and commanded Carol to give up her belief in predestination and to move back home. Paul and Carol were devastated. They had grown very close and were strongly considering engagement. They longed to have Glen's approval, but he would not even speak with Paul. Carol moved home for a few months to try to patch things up with her parents, but they were unwilling to listen to her appeals.

Paul and Carol then sought help and counsel from their pastor who contacted Glen and tried to reason with him. Glen admitted that Paul had conducted himself as a gentleman and that he had no objection other than Paul's doctrine. "I don't want my grandchildren being raised to be little Calvinists," he said. When the pastor encouraged Glen to let Carol make her own choice, Glen told the pastor, "The Bible says that children must obey their parents. She is my daughter, and I have the right to tell her whom she can and cannot marry, and I don't have to give any other reason or explain myself!" When the pastor suggested that Glen might be provoking his daughter to anger by his unreasonableness (Eph. 6:4), Glen warned the pastor, "If you encourage them to marry or perform their marriage, you will have participated in stealing my daughter away from me and the curses of God will fall upon you and your ministry." Glen also told Carol that if she married Paul, the entire family would have nothing to do with her ever again. What should Paul, Carol, and the pastor do now? How would you advise Paul?

The trauma we feel upon giving up our kids in marriage has been exquisitely portrayed in many movies and plays. The musical *Fiddler on the Roof* lets us in to the mind of papa Tevye as he suffers through the marriages of each of his five daughters, watching as each one chooses to move farther and farther from his own wishes for them. At one point during the play he and his wife look at each other and wonder what happened to their little ones . . . just when did they grow to be adults?

134

Many of us know how this feels and although sometimes we're really glad that they're marrying, we can't believe it's happening already.

On the other hand, movies such as *Failure to Launch* point out the painfully humorous difficulties that result when our kids don't move out and get married as they should. Whether we think it's coming too soon or too late, or if we wish that we could pick their partner for them, our kids' marriages are generally difficult for us. Let's take a few moments now to consider some of the factors that may be making this hard time of transition even more complex.

### Whose Dream?

Many mothers pray from the moment their children are born that they will find godly spouses. They dream of the day when their husband will walk their virgin Christian daughter, dressed in a beautiful, white gown, down the aisle of their church to be given in marriage to a fine young Christian man of whom they fully approve (perhaps the son of their close friend). In their dream, their daughter's fiancé is a godly, pure young man who is a wonderful provider for her. Both daughter and fiancé want lots of kids and plan to live in their neighborhood so that they could help raise their grandchildren. Perhaps their daughter's husband would even get involved in the family's business. These were the dreams that may have filled your heart as you rocked your little one to sleep.

Sadly, at least for some of us, dreams vanish before they ever really get going. Our children make romantic choices that are beyond our control and that we may not like. Learning how to respond to our disappointments in a godly way is key to maintaining a strong relationship with them—even when they've (inadvertently) shattered all our dreams.

## *Whose Choice Is It Anyway?*

Parental conflict over their children's romantic choices is certainly not a new phenomenon. Shakespeare's famous play *Romeo and Juliet* portrays the timeless tragedy of young lovers whose parents don't approve of their desire to marry.[1] We believe that it is ideal for children to seek their parents' wisdom and oversight as they choose a life partner. We're also aware that there are many problems with how dating is done in our contemporary culture, problems that lead to immorality and heartbreak (minimarriages that end in minidivorces). Parents frequently have keen insight into problems, while our kids are blinded by "love" and rush headlong into permanent relationships. Charm and beauty can obscure wise discernment and young adults are notorious for falling in love for the wrong reasons.

As counselors, we've seen a number of young people rescued from unsuitable relationships by heeding the wise counsel of loving parents. For instance, twenty-year-old Leah was originally furious when her father, Stephen, asked her to stop seeing her boyfriend, Dave. It turned out that her dad had twice caught Dave looking at Internet porn when he was visiting their home. Stephen was also concerned about Dave's anger problem. Because Leah respected her father's judgment and took a break from the relationship, over time she was able to see Dave's immaturity for herself and was thankful for a father who was willing to take a stand to protect her.

We appreciate many aspects of the courtship model where parents seek to guide their children through the all-important process of choosing a spouse. We think it is good for an adult child to seek the protection and oversight of her parents in her relationships with young men, especially when she is younger. Parents may be able to identify challenges a young couple might face or potential character issues in a prospective partner.[2] We also think that it is ideal for a young person not to be involved in numerous romantic relationships prior to marriage, but rather to guard the body and the heart so that he or she can enter into marriage in purity. It certainly would be ideal if everyone from both families would agree about the timing and location of the wedding, the choice of bridesmaids' dresses, and the china patterns. But few of us receive what is ideal in this fallen world.

## The "Of Age" Principle

We recognize that there is some disagreement among Christians as to the degree of authority parents have to encourage or forbid the marriage of their children. Chapter 1 explains the biblical basis for our belief that when a young person is "of age" he or she becomes primarily responsible for his or her own choices in life. We believe that this principle changes the nature of the relationship between parent and child from one of obedience and control to one of respect and counsel.

Because we believe that the Bible teaches this principle, we do not think that parents have the right to impose a marriage partner on their child. Even in biblical times, when women had few rights, they did get to choose whom they wished to marry. When Abraham's servant sought a wife for Isaac, Rebekah was asked by her family members if she was willing to go back to marry Isaac.[3] In Numbers 36:6, the Lord allowed the daughters of Zelophehad to "marry whom they wish" within their father's family (NASB). In 1 Corinthians 7:39, Paul teaches that a widow is free to "be married to whom she wishes, only in the Lord" (NASB). Paul does not say that she is only free to marry the man her father or her brothers choose.

137

We know that some well-meaning teachers argue for parental control from 1 Corinthians 7:36–38. They do so because in some translations it seems to say that a father has authority to determine when or if his virgin daughter marries. Actually, the word *daughter* does not appear in the original text. Given that the context addresses one's personal choice of whether or not to marry, we believe that this verse is better understood to refer to one's *betrothed*, as the ESV translates it.[4] We agree that parental approval is ideal, but we do not think that it is mandated in every case.

### Does Daddy Always Know Best?

An article entitled "Daddy's Girl: Courtship and a Father's Rights" argues that daughters are actually *owned* by their fathers because of their rights as progenitor to do as they wish with what they have made.[5] According to this understanding, "the will of the father regarding his daughter IS the will of God."[6] There also have been other teachers who have taught almost absolute parental authority over the marital choices of their children, especially daughters. Another teacher goes so far as to say that "God can bless no marriage which takes place without parental consent" and warns that mutigenerational curses will fall upon the couple who marry against their parents' will (even if the parents are unbelievers).[7] While we agree that the ideal and the norm should be that parents are in full agreement with their children's marital choices, we believe that those who teach that parents have authority to make these choices go beyond Scripture.[8]

But what if daddy is a Muslim and won't approve of his Christian daughter marrying a fellow believer? Or what if mommy and daddy selfishly want to keep their daughter at home to meet their needs, rather than allowing her to enjoy a family of her own? One daughter writes of her parents,

> Their plan for me was my remaining single, living at home with them, getting a doctorate . . . and eventually working from their home. . . . As those who have known my parents have said, all of this was not about my fiancé, but what he represented: my parents' losing unchallenged control over my life. They had envisioned my life as an outgrowth of theirs, which necessitated that I remain unmarried, childless, and fully dependent under their roof.

What if mommy and daddy are abusively controlling and are unwilling to let their daughter marry any man they can't control? We respectfully disagree with the premise underlying this teaching. Daddy doesn't always know best.

The Bible teaches that there are limits to all human authority, including parental authority. All human authority is under God's authority, whose infallible Word is our supreme authority. When the apostles declared, "we must obey God rather than men" (Acts 5:29, NASB), they were defining the limits of human authority by defying their religious leaders. Their resistance proves that there are times when we have not only the freedom, but the obligation, to resist unbiblical abuses of authority.

Even if you remain convinced that your child is not free to court or marry without your permission, you do not have the power to control her choices. You may object, "But when she was twelve her daddy gave her a promise ring and she pledged never to court or marry without her father's permission." Such rings may convey a good message about the ideal relationship between a father and daughter. However, we are not sure that it is reasonable for a parent to demand that a twenty-three-year-old daughter keep a pledge she made when she was a little girl and had no idea of how she would view life as an adult. Nor does it give license to a father to abuse his authority by being unreasonably controlling.

Rather than trying to gain control with brute force, parents would be much wiser to win influence with their daughters and sons through gracious love. If you do not have your child's heart, you will have little influence in her choice of a spouse, regardless of your understanding of your authority or the promises she made when young.

### She May Say "I Do" Even if You Say "Don't"

Again, the ideal is that young people marry with the blessing of their parents. A marriage that takes place without parental approval is a very sad exception, but parents have to recognize that their children have the right to choose their own life partners. If parents object for less than valid biblical reasons, the child still has the freedom to marry whom she will.

We've seen many heartbreaking abuses of parental authority. We have seen parents try to stop a marriage because of their prejudice against the family background of the fiancée. One set of parents objected because the proposed marriage partner was not physically attractive enough for their child. Another mother sought to break her daughter's engagement, not because of any issue of sin, but because she claimed that God had supernaturally told her that the relationship must end. Other parents refuse to give a reason, but simply try to stop their child's marriage by raw authority. A young wife wrote to us about her experience with her parents.

There was no allowance made for conscience—my duty was to believe exactly as my parents did until they approved of a suitor that had the exact same doctrinal beliefs as them.

140

My husband and I were actually told during one of our pre-marriage discussions with my dad that I was not allowed to believe differently than he did; that it was my duty to obey my parents and not to arrive at an understanding based on my own conscience. That is truly what sealed the deal for us in terms of proceeding in marriage without his blessing.

God expects those to whom he has given authority to use their position to serve those under their care, even as Jesus used his authority to serve us (Mark 10:45; John 13:3–20).

We strongly encourage young people whose parents object to their courtship or engagement to make every effort to understand and evaluate their parents' concerns and to strive to gain parental approval. We respect those who have gone so far as to delay their plans for marriage in hopes that their parents would come around. We encourage them to seek the counsel and help of pastors and other church leaders to mediate in such situations. Often there is fault on both sides and, if one side would humbly confess their sin and seek forgiveness (Matt. 7:3–5), reconciliation could take place. We have been disappointed to see both young people and parents who stubbornly held their ground, refusing to make the necessary efforts to work out their differences (or to give their dreams to God).

When a young couple believe they have done everything possible to seek peace with their parents (Rom. 12:18) but without result, we encourage them to seek counsel and accountability from church authorities, and possibly other family members, before moving ahead. We have seen cases in which church leaders have agreed that the young people have done all that they can do and have participated in their marriage.[9] If their church leaders also have objections and concerns about their relationship, we would strongly encourage the young couple to try to understand and address these issues before getting married.

We have also watched while other family members (especially grandparents) have stepped in to offer wise counsel and help when the parents have failed to be supportive. One woman writes about how her grandparents encouraged her in a difficult situation.

> My grandparents called to affirm me . . . in my relationship with Caleb. They told me that they were proud of me and that I always had been a mature, responsible, good young woman, and that at twenty-three, I was old enough to determine what was God's best for my life. God blessed our wedding day incredibly by showering us with profound and unexpected family support. Unsolicited, relatives and friends on my side offered their familial and emotional support for us at every turn. As a particularly special gift from God, my grandfather, the patriarch of the family, made it exceedingly clear on behalf of the rest of my relatives that they joyfully supported my new life with Caleb and were proud of me.

## When Their Dreams and Ours Collide

It is hard to imagine anything more emotionally trying than to see our children making foolish romantic choices. Many godly parents have suffered terribly as they watched their adult children involving themselves with people who seemed totally unsuitable for marriage. They have seen their children follow the world into both heterosexual and homosexual immorality. They also have seen their children enter into marriages that appeared doomed from the start. But because we are dealing with "of age" adults rather than dependent children, our response to their choices, heartbreaking as they may be, must remain loving and respectful.

We are aware that some leaders teach that parents should shun their children if they disobey their wishes or go against their particular understanding of Scripture. They would also say that parents should refuse to have any contact with their child's significant other if they do not approve. Furthermore, disapproving parents should refuse to attend the wedding, and once the couple is married, they should have nothing to do with them until they admit that they were wrong. Such parents often carry the shunning a step further and demand that all other family members also shun their rebellious child,[10] or else they too will be shunned. We have heard of cases in which parents have removed all photos of the offending child from the home.[11] Such an approach is contrary to Scripture and is often motivated by pride and vengeful anger over shattered personal dreams, rather than the pursuit of biblical righteousness (Rom.12:19; James 1:19–20). Even if your child is wrong, it may be years or decades before he will agree with you, if at all. In the meantime, you've lost the opportunity to love and serve him.

## We Are Free to Love and Welcome

The Bible teaches that we are free to love people who have sinned against us.[12] Without this liberty we wouldn't be able to love anyone at all, since everyone we know will sin against us in some way eventually. Jesus taught that we should emulate God by loving our enemies (Matt. 5:43–48). Of course, he not only taught this, but he also lived it out for us, by laying down his life for us and calling us "friends" when we hated him. Paul declared that we should do everything within our power to be at peace with all men and overcome the evil done to us by doing good to others (Rom. 12:18–21). We should never bitterly shun those who have wronged us.[13]

In light of the gospel and God's great love for us while we were still in our sin, we can show genuine love and care for others, particularly those of whom we disapprove. We can try to understand them and try to comprehend what attracts our child to her significant other. By remembering the gospel message, that we are both sinful and flawed yet loved and welcomed, we can welcome this uninvited visitor warmly. When you keep the doors open, you're helping your own cause because this uninvited visitor will view you as a friend and perhaps even a counselor. No one wants to take counsel from someone who really doesn't like them. If you openly welcome your child's new friend, you will remove the pressure of disapproval, and your child may then actually invite your counsel.

When our kids don't think they have to defend their position to us, they're freer to look at what they're doing and admit that they may be making a mistake. But when we turn the discussion into a fight for control, we may be inadvertently forcing them to defend a position they aren't very committed to. One wise mom told her son, who was involved with someone she thought was less than ideal, "We can live near anyone you can live with." She explains her approach in this way, "What we tried to avoid during this entire time was the mistake we had seen other families make: an insistence on pure obedience from a twenty-year-old young man as opposed to showing respect for his manhood. . . . We tried to influence but not demand obedience, believing the decision was his."

Words said to or about a person who may become your son- or daughter-in-law are hard to forget and may damage your relationships for years to come. As one wise dad wrote, "We want to know our grandchildren. Whether or not we approve of our son/daughter-in-law, we will make the best that we can of our relationship for the sake of our child and grandchildren." If your child marries someone you disapprove of, you should still attend the wedding to show your commitment to help make their marriage a success.[14] Your refusal to go may create rifts in your relationship with the new couple and potentially with your extended family,[15] which could last decades.

While we cannot control our child's romantic choices, we shouldn't be an enabler of sin either. Because homosexuality is a mockery of God's design for marriage, it would be wrong for you to participate in a homosexual wedding. Likewise, if a child is in a sexually immoral relationship, we may allow him and his friend to stay in our home when visiting from out of town, but not to sleep in the same room. Of course, if this offends them, they can pay for their own hotel room. Likewise, when visiting them, we can stay in a hotel rather than in their home. Paul gives a useful guideline in Romans 14:23, "Whatever is not from faith is sin" (NASB).

### When They're Still Waiting for Their Dreams to Come True

We opened this chapter talking about Tevye, the father in *Fiddler on the Roof.* One of the other characters in the play is the Matchmaker, whose job it is to "make matches" and "catch catches." While it's fine for us to identify with Tevye or his wife, it's not fine for us to identify with the Matchmaker and push our single adult children too hard toward marriage. Again, we don't know God's plan for our kids' lives. It may be that he is calling them to a season or even a lifetime of singleness (1 Cor. 7:1, 8, 32–33). Or it may be that they are not yet ready to take on the responsibilities of marriage. As much as we may be sure that we know the perfect one for our son or daughter, we should be patient and very hesitant about pushing them toward someone. Lastly, even if we think we've accurately identified the shortcomings that are inhibiting our child's success with the opposite sex, he would probably prefer that you not point them out.

## *Our Dream and God's Gracious Choice*

When it comes to our adult children's romantic choices, we must accept the fact that we are not in control. On a human level it's obvious that our kids will make their own decisions . . . even though we had *such good plans!* Ultimately, we know that God is sovereign and is working out his plan for them and for us. His plan may not coincide exactly with our dream, but we can trust that it is the best plan (Rom. 8:28). Perhaps you're suffering right now as you think of how your dreams have been shattered by your child's romantic choices. Even so, we know that for those who love him, God works out everything for good. We can also trust that he'll work this situation out in that way too. We can trust him because he "did not spare his own Son but gave him up for us all." In this scenario, we're the tainted bride that the pure Son pursues. And although it was the Father's will for him to pursue us, Jesus is the one who was shunned on Calvary because of his love for us. Now, in light of his suffering, we can trust that "with him" God will also "graciously give us all things" (Rom. 8:32). You can find strength today in remembering that God's good plan is that you become more and more like Christ through this time of suffering. He's fitting you with your beautiful wedding gown, making you trust him, and transforming your character. As you find strength in the Lord you can show forth his peace to your kids—and to their spouses. Remember, you can "do all things through him who strengthens [you]" (Phil. 4:13).

## Let's Talk More about It

1. *Christianity Today* published a cover story in the August 2009 issue entitled "The Case for Early Marriage," in

which sociologist Mark Regnerus expressed concern that young evangelicals are postponing marriage until their late twenties or early thirties. He argued that changes in our culture have caused it to take longer for our kids to complete their training and become financially independent.

Part of the solution he proposed is to encourage young people to marry at an earlier age, and for their parents to offer financial help (for example to complete their education) to make this possible.[16] While the ideal may still be that our children wait to marry until they are financially self-sufficient, there are other considerations, not the least of which is the sexual temptations they will face if they wait. Young people who are otherwise mature enough to handle the responsibilities of marriage may be better off to go ahead and get married, rather than trying to survive their twenties as singles. Albert Mohler[17] and John Piper[18] have also suggested that early marriage may be best for many Christians in their twenties, even if they are still in school.

Parents who in the past have said that their kids are on their own once they are married may want to reconsider their stance. We recognize that there are many dangers both from the standpoint of parents using money to control their kids and young people getting married before they are mature enough to take on their marital roles. On the other hand, we also believe that there are cases in which the benefits outweigh the risks. What is your response to this perspective?

2.  Have you struggled with a child's choice of intimate friend or spouse? How have you responded? Has your response been gospel centered and left the door open

for relationship? Why or why not? If not, what steps can you take now to try to establish a relationship?

3. How does the sacrifice of the Bridegroom impact your perspective about your child's choices? Do you see yourself as the impure, sullied bride? Do you understand how Jesus had to be shunned on Calvary so that you never would be? How does that influence your acceptance of your daughter- or son-in-law?

4. Summarize what you've learned in this chapter in four or five sentences.

# 10

# Your New Math: Adding by Subtracting

THE DAY HAS FINALLY COME: she's finally married. After the wedding, you and your spouse return to your once full house and begin to think that this solitude will define your lives from then on. But suddenly there are luncheons with in-laws, and holiday tables are added to include at least two more families—your kid's family and your new friends the in-laws. And then the grandkids come! Although it might seem that the marriage of our child strips us of relationships, in reality it usually doubles or even triples them. The truth is that their marriage doesn't remove relationships, but rather adds them. And, of course, every new relationship brings new and troublesome challenges. Now, instead of facing the simple challenges we've always faced as a family, we've got the challenges that other families face too. How involved will the new in-laws be? Who gets the kids for Thanksgiving? How many hours do we get the grandkids in comparison with the in-laws?

Anthony was very happy to have finally found and married Cely after many years of loneliness. But he was shocked when a month after their marriage he found himself even less lonely when Cely's mother and father sold their belongings, quit their jobs, and moved into Anthony and Cely's small condo. Cely's family is from a culture in which it is customary for children to honor their parents by inviting them into their home, so that the mother can help her daughter learn her domestic duties and ultimately help with the grandchildren. Anthony objected to the loss of privacy and told Cely that it would be better for them to have the place to themselves. Cely pleaded, "We can't just send my parents away. It just isn't done. I will be disgraced in the eyes of my family." How involved should we parents be in the lives of our married kids?

Hank and Jen have a different kind of problem. They had always enjoyed a good relationship with their son Brian, though he was often very quiet. But after Brian married Kathleen, they felt like their relationship with their son disappeared. When they would phone, he would say very little and quickly have to go. When they invited Brian and Kathleen to come visit, they would refuse. During the holidays, the tension was so thick that it overshadowed the festivities. Finally, on Christmas Eve, their daughter-in-law told Hank and Jen off. Kathleen stated that she and Brian were sick and tired of Hank and Jen trying to control them. Furthermore, they had determined that they weren't going to be pressured any more. If Hank and Jen didn't back off, there would be no relationship. While Kathleen was talking, Brian just sat looking down at the floor. When Kathleen was done, Hank and Jen simply went back to their room in stunned silence and wept. How should we handle breaks in relationship like this?

## Avoiding Conflicts in These New Relationships

In-law conflict is a popular subject for comedians, but their attempts at humor are rooted in reality. A quick scan of newspaper advice columns makes this clear. Wayne Mack, in his excellent booklet "In-laws: Married with Parents,"[1] provides research that shows how relationships with in-laws can affect the quality of a marriage, not only in its early stages, but even for people who have been married for a long time. He also points out that in-law problems are not new. Isaac's wife, Rebekah, had issues with the wives of her son Esau (Gen. 26:34–35). Jacob had major problems with his father-in-law, Laban. David's father-in-law, Saul, tried to kill him. Jesus also warns that the gospel will cause divisions in family relationships, including in-law relationships (Luke 12:51–53). On the positive side, Moses was greatly helped by his father-in-law, Jethro (Ex. 18), and Jesus healed Simon Peter's mother-in-law (Luke 4:38–39).

The Bible teaches that our child's marriage creates a new family unit (Gen. 2:24). For some of us this dramatic change in relationship with our children is a very difficult adjustment. It's just hard to let go. We want to try to influence or control their choices regarding education, career, family planning, church involvement, investments, and home purchases. Some of our kids feel caught in the middle when the holidays come around because they can't be in three places at once. They feel pressure from both sides of the family, plus they want to start their own family traditions. Some newlyweds start out trying to please everyone. But after a few years of frustration, they overreact in the opposite direction and pull far away from both families.

A key to success in in-law relationships is to recognize that marriage is the most important human relationship. All other relationships are subordinate. When we put our marriages first, our kids will benefit from our example by learning the importance of putting their own spouses first. Since Scripture so clearly states that married children are to form their own family unit, by implication we're commanded to allow them to do so. Although we may be tempted to try to control our child even at the expense of his relationship with his spouse, we've got to resist that temptation. If we don't, we may find them moving far from us to preserve their marriage, or we may be culpable for problems in their home. Our kids are to be primarily concerned with pleasing their spouses (1 Cor. 7:33–34), not us. You can only have as much of a relationship with your married kids as they choose to offer you. As you treat them with love and respect, trust will grow.

A new couple, coming from two different family backgrounds, will need room to work through their own convictions, preferences, and traditions together, rather than simply adopting their parents' perspectives. Think back to when you and your spouse were first married and remember how defensive and sensitive you felt when your parents criticized you. What we may mean as well-intentioned advice may be received as disapproving criticism accompanied by extreme pressure. For this reason, we urge you to make a general rule of waiting to be invited before offering your advice. One parent advises, "Keep your mouth closed! Only break the glass if there is a fire! There is a threshold that you must not step over. You cannot do anything that would be conceived of as trying to build a wedge between your child and their spouse. Their marriage is sacred."

152

Rather than sinfully criticizing our son- or daughter-in-law to our child[2], we should look for things to commend and treat them as an equal in our family. One parent writes, "I want my child's spouse to feel like they've been part of the family for years. The spouse is normally starting out as an outsider, so I would make an extra effort to reach out to them, use endearing nicknames we use for our other children, and tell them how glad we are to have them in the family."

It also is important to realize that we will probably have different relationships with different in-laws. One daughter-in-law may feel very comfortable calling us mom or dad, while a son-in-law may need time for trust and relationship to grow. Like our kids, we've got to learn the ground rules for these new relationships, remembering that our primary goal is to support and nurture their relationship.[3] Finally, because there is so much conflict in in-law relationships, we need all the wisdom God offers in his Word to help us to strive for "peace with everyone" (Heb. 12:14). (In his wonderful book *The Peacemaker*,[4] Ken Sande expounds the biblical teaching on peacemaking. In order to assist you as you work through conflicts with your in-laws, we've summarized a few of his principles in appendix A.)

While some conflicts are inevitable, many parents enjoy wonderful relationships with their children and their spouses. It can be a great joy to see our kids building their own families. They honor us when they imitate what they appreciated about our family traditions and seek our counsel as they face major decisions. One dad writes, "One of the greatest lessons has been what surprisingly great friends our married kids and their spouses have turned out to be. We enjoy their adult friendship more than any other friendships we've ever experienced! This is truly a surprising gift from God!"

## Blessed Grandparenting

I was exceptionally blessed to have strong relationships with three of my grandparents. I especially remember spending a lot of time with my maternal grandfather as I was growing up. When I was young I would often spend the night at his house and he would tell me great cowboy stories.[5] As I got a bit older he was passionate about turning me into a hunter and training me how to safely use firearms. Looking back, I still marvel at all he did for us grandkids. After he retired he bought a small ranch in South Texas and seemed to spend all of his time turning it into a magnet to draw in his grandchildren. He bought a horse for us to ride, stocked a pond in which we could fish for bass, and did everything humanly possible to lure a big buck deer onto his property for when I would visit during hunting season. I remember sitting with him for hours in deer blinds talking about every subject under the sun. He always had time for me and had boundless interest in everything in my life. Through those conversations he instilled values in me that continue to be foundational in my life. Perhaps the greatest effect he had on me was his example, especially as a husband. He treated my grandmother like a queen. I remember marveling at my six-foot-two-inch grandfather, after a long day of hard work, doing the dishes each night, insisting that my grandmother rest after having made such a wonderful meal. I cannot imagine who I would be today if not for the influence of my grandfather.

### Adding Even More Blessings!

Becoming a grandparent is probably one of the most emotional experiences in life. On the one hand we tell ourselves, "I am much too young to be a grandparent. My grandparents were really old when I was a kid." On the other hand it is

154

thrilling to see the beginnings of a new generation. From the first time we set our eyes on those little bundles, we feel an incredible bond with our grandchildren. When we were raising our own children we were frequently too busy to enjoy them and too inexperienced to know what to do. Grandkids are fun because now we get a chance to enjoy their childhood while not having all of the exhausting responsibilities of parenting. Of course, the Scriptures tell us how wonderful grandchildren can be, calling them the "crown of the aged" (Prov. 17:6), and how just seeing them is a rich blessing from God (Ps. 128:6).

### We're to Be a Blessing to Them Too

The greatest blessing we can give our grandchildren is a spiritual one, making his great works known to our "children and our children's children" (Deut. 4:9).[6] One grandmother, Lois, imparted faith to her daughter and then to her grandson, Timothy, and she's commended for it (2 Tim. 1:5). The Lord may use your words to powerfully impact your child's spiritual life. We're sure Lois didn't know how God would use her love for young Timothy, but just think how he did.

Many Christian grandparents whose children are not believers have opportunity to be a spiritual influence on their grandchildren. They may allow their children to attend church with us and wouldn't mind us reading Bible stories to them. Such a privilege should be cherished and handled with care, avoiding any criticism of the parents' lack of spiritual interest. One of the greatest challenges faced by some grandparents is when their non-Christian children forbid them to influence their grandkids toward Christ through reading the Bible, praying with them, or taking them to church. As hard as this is, it seems best to submit to the authority your kids have over their minor children simply because, if we defy their rules, we may lose any access to our grandchildren. Keep loving and praying and see what God may do.

What an opportunity we have as grandparents! Rather than get wrapped up in more selfish pursuits, if we're able, we should take every advantage to be involved in their lives. We can attend their recitals and their baseball and soccer games. Even if they don't live close by, we can send letters, emails, small gifts, and even photos. We can remember every birthday and share with them how the Lord has saved and changed our lives. A son remembers, "I have many fond memories spending quality time with my grandparents. They make up some of the best memories of my childhood."

### Seek to Bless Your Children

Although we should be reluctant to offer unsolicited advice to our grown children, parenthood often motivates them to come to us (sometimes in desperation) for help and wisdom. "How do you potty train a two-year-old boy who just doesn't care?" "What do you do when your fourteen-year-old daughter wants to go out on a date?" Suddenly they realize that raising kids isn't as easy as it once looked. As they walk through the difficulties of raising children, they may begin to appreciate what we did for them and perhaps even see how their actions may have hurt us when they were in our home.

As grandparents, our help is most often appreciated when we babysit so that our kids and their spouses can spend needed romantic time alone on dates or during a weekend getaway. Although watching the kids is tough, the truth is that we enjoy our quality time with them about as much as they enjoy being with us. Grandmothers can offer to help around the house when there is a new baby or when circumstances are particularly difficult. Some grandparents have the privilege of participating directly in the educating of their grandchildren by schooling them in particular subjects, taking their grandchildren on field trips, or teaching them important practical skills.

Often when both parents work, grandparents are called upon to watch the grandkids. "Among the 11.3 million children younger than five whose mothers were employed, 30 percent were cared for on a regular basis by a grandparent during their mother's working hours."[7] Although caring for our grandchildren can be a great blessing to both them and us, both parents and grandparents need to be sensitive to each other. The parents need to be careful to not presumptuously take advantage of the grandparents, and the grandparents should not be pushy in offering help nor be offended when their offers are declined.

We all have dreams and desires about what we would like to do with our grandchildren, but grandparents can only be as involved in the lives of their grandchildren as their parents allow them to be. Any plans you want to make with your grandchildren must be cleared with their parents, without becoming pushy or presumptuous. This shows respect for their right to raise their children as they see fit.

We also must respect their obligation to raise their children according to their own conscience and convictions, remembering that the Lord has put them in charge of our grandkids (Eph. 6:1–3). If they decide to teach your grandchildren that Santa Claus is real, you don't have the right to tell them otherwise. On the other hand, we might cause significant problems at Christmas time by insisting that Santa was real when our kids don't want their children to participate in the Santa myth.

Although all grandparents know that it's part of their DNA to spoil their grandchildren, we've got to be very careful not to give gifts or take our grandkids to any event that their parents might object to. We need to follow their parents' rules and address questions of discipline in the manner they tell us. In doing this, we'll be teaching our grandchildren that they should respect and submit to their parents' authority too. Or as one grandmother told us, "Nobody wants to have their children returned with the attitude, 'I'd rather be at Grandma's because she lets me do what I want, and you won't!'" Some parents give the grandparents the freedom to spank their kids when they're in their care while others do not. This is one of those places where good communication is vital. Be sure to ask your child *before* the kids are in your care what kind of discipline they think would be appropriate. Remember, if we haven't been given permission to spank a child, then we do not have the authority to do so, and we may end up forfeiting our babysitting privileges if we insist. If our grandkids become unmanageable because we can't discipline them, we have the right to set limits on the circumstances in which we're willing to watch them.

### But What if We're Not Allowed to See Them?

We have counseled grandparents who have had access to the children cut off or severely limited. Whenever we face any difficulty, especially when we believe we're being sinned against, we should seek to identify what beams may be in our own eye (Matt. 7:3–5). We should question whether we have failed in some way to respect the parents' wishes. We know of young moms and dads who have been extremely frustrated with how their parents have pushed limits and even gone against their rules with the grandkids. Some have even been carelessly dismissive of parental standards. Rather than blaming our kids for these difficulties, we should seek to understand how we may have offended them and seek their forgiveness. Humility and loving submission to their restrictions will go a long way in rebuilding their trust.

## *When Grandparents Become Substitute Parents*

According to government estimates, there are approximately 5.7 million grandchildren being raised by their grandparents.[8] Sometimes this occurs when the parents die. Occasionally a widowed or divorced daughter moves back in with her parents to get help with the kids, perhaps allowing her to go to work. Sometimes the parents simply aren't willing or able to raise their own kids. Many of us know grandparents who are raising a grandchild whose unwed mother either isn't responsible enough to care for her child (perhaps because of drugs or alcohol), or simply doesn't want to do so. We have also seen cases in which a young couple divorces, but both want to be free to sow their wild oats, and are completely willing to let their parents step up to raise their children. While the circumstances behind these cases are usually tragic, this could be a significant opportunity to train a grandchild, who would otherwise have been raised in a very worldly way, in the fear and admonition of the Lord. We think that it is wonderful that grandparents are willing to sacrifice what should be their more peaceful empty-nest years for the good of their own flesh and blood.

Grandparents who choose to raise their grandchildren should count the cost in terms of time, energy, and finances. Your grandchildren will be approaching the rocking teen years about the time you feel ready for the rocking chair, although their presence may keep you young. By far the biggest problem we have seen in these situations is that after the grandparents have poured their lives into their grandchild for several years, one of the parents, who had been irresponsible and disengaged up until then, decides that he or she wants the child back. The grandparents, having sought to train their grandchild biblically, are deeply troubled to think of the unsaved worldly parent taking over. Often a nasty legal tug of war ensues. When grandparents are asked to raise a grandchild, we advise them to require a written agreement that transfers legal authority of the grandchild to them. If the grandparents are going to take on parental responsibility, it must be accompanied by parental authority. This may also cause the parents to reconsider their choices to abandon their duties to their children.

### Grandparenting Your Adult Grandchildren

When our grandchildren reach adulthood, we're then able to relate to them as fellow adults. The restrictions that may have been imposed upon us by their parents while they were still minors will no longer apply. For example, if we had been forbidden to speak to them about the Lord, we are now free to seek to have a godly influence upon them. We have seen Christian grandfathers become mentors to their young adult grandsons. We have also seen grandparents step in to help their grandchildren through hard times with their parents. If the opportunity arises to participate in this kind of dispute, however, be aware of how it may affect your relationship with both your child and your grandchild. Make sure to think biblically if you decide to take a side.

### Faithful Living in Our New Families

At first blush, it seems as though releasing a son or daughter to marriage would eventuate in our solitude. But in our discussion we've seen something entirely different happening. As the old saying goes, we haven't lost a son, we've gained a daughter . . . and her parents, siblings, friends, and children . . . and our children's children! Rather than seeing our family shrink in size, we've witnessed a population explosion. And what an explosion of opportunities! Although relationships always bring occasions for conflict, sorrow, and sin, they also open the door to a greater fruitfulness that may affect generations to come. Each one opens the door for us to grow in love for our neighbor and to spread the wonderful news of a Savior who loves his big family and delights in blessing it through each one of us.

### Let's Talk More about It

1. How would you characterize your relationship(s) with your daughter- or son-in-law? Are you aware of any ways in which you have failed to respect your child's marital relationship? Do you need to take any action now to right those wrongs?

2. How would you characterize your relationship(s) with your grandchildren? Are you aware of any ways in which you have failed to respect your children's wishes with them? Do you favor one set of grandkids over another? Do you need to take any action now to right those wrongs?

3. If you're experiencing any conflict with anyone in these relationships, please turn to appendix A and prayerfully consider how you should respond.

4. Summarize what you've learned in this chapter in four or five sentences.

# Conclusion

# It Still Hurts Because You Never Stop Being a Parent

WE ALL STARTED our journey as parents with such high expectations. We were sure that we would do better than our folks did and that our kids would turn out better than we did. For many of us, as our children matured and reached adulthood, we realized that our dreams were not going to be realized. As one dad wrote, "Of all of the challenges of dealing with our adult kids, I think the largest personal struggle that I have had to deal with is the disappointment." He continued, "My wife and I are still fumbling through this stuff, with some successes and some failures. The one area that we continue to see weakness in is our ability to trust God for our adult kids. Nothing in life has tested my faith more than the unbelief of my own sons." John Piper echoed this sentiment when he poignantly wrote, "A son is not a father's only life-investment, but there is none like it, and when it fails, there is no sorrow like this sorrow."[1]

### Your Kids Belong to the Lord

John Calvin, writing almost five hundred years ago, addresses the issue of our total dependence upon God's sovereign grace working in our families.

> It is certainly true that fathers of families and heads of houses ought to be careful to do their duty in governing those who are placed under their authority. But the main thing that parents should do is to take refuge in God. Those who have children should realize that they will never reach their goal and their pain can produce no good fruit unless God takes the whole matter in hand and controls it. . . . Even when a man has only his wife he must know that when his house is not blessed by God there will be nothing but poverty.[2]

While we are responsible to follow God's Word in training our children when they are young and in seeking to be a godly influence on them as they mature, ultimately God is our only refuge. He is in control and he alone can bring forth good fruit in our families. We must entrust our children to him. One wise mom tells of her switch from fear to freedom:

> Before your child is born you begin your parenting journey with great hope and desire to keep the Lord's admonition to raise your children up in him. But somewhere along the way, your mindset changes and you begin to believe that the desired outcome of your children depends on you. I might add that the desired, honorable outcome is to have loving, godly children. Though I would say that through my years of parenting as I would seek the Lord and pray that

I would have the grace to do this; I felt disillusioned and frustrated when I saw that God's plan differed from what I had imagined it would look like, and I wondered why. As I began to seek the Lord in this, I realized that somewhere along the way, what I had pictured for my daughter did not come to complete fruition. I realized that I had made an idol of what I wanted to have in her character and had not been prayerfully open to what God had intended for our girl. I did want God's best, but my response to the reality of what God designed did not reflect an openness or joy. Praise God for his illuminating goodness! It is his plan, not mine. It is for his glory, not my satisfaction.

I wanted to have an open hand to the Lord by remembering Job, "the Lord gives and the Lord takes away, blessed be the name of the Lord." This open-handed idea frees me from feeling that I am responsible for the outcome of circumstances that my children are deciding on. I totally release them to the Lord who is sovereign. He knows and is overseeing every aspect of their lives. . . . Somewhere along the way, I felt that I had to be the one controlling every aspect. Otherwise I thought, "Oh no! They might end up doing something irrevocable or detrimental." Yes, they might, but God knows about that too. At this stage of life with adult children, this is not my burden to take up. God has a plan for each of them. I am only the messenger, the ambassador. The outcome belongs to the Lord. I really have a sense of freedom having this attitude. The other idea is that I don't have to know everything that they are into, who they are with, or where they are going, because the omniscient, omnipresent Lord knows. I don't have to take up that "burden" (so to speak) which belongs to him. Therefore I am really free to focus on building the relationship and at peace to trust God to work out his perfect will.

I believe that the biggest mistake I have made is parenting out of fear. I thought that if I didn't correct everything and anything I saw that could possibly become an issue in the future, I would be held accountable or liable for allowing them to get wrapped up in a habitual sin. This caused me to become uptight, worrisome, and angry, all of which have contributed to a strained, imbalanced relationship. This is the complete opposite of the loving relationship I desired to have with my children. . . . God has already decided who are his. Remembering this frees me from worry and anxiety and protects me from feeling the need to bring correction or truth constantly or in a heavy way. I am totally free to rest on the Lord and be open to his leading, as I pray and wait for direction and wisdom. I try to prepare myself before I have encounters with them, asking the Lord to remind me of anything from our previous encounters that may be important to bring up now. The rest I leave with the Lord by his grace. . . . Knowing and resting on God's faithfulness and in his design of the particular troubles that have come into our lives makes my heart surrender and wait patiently on him. There is no use fighting against it, worrying about it, ignoring it, or wishing it away. He has allowed it and he will provide a way to go through it. And since there is nothing new under the sun, I don't have to wonder why this is happening to us or what people will think. I can have joy and peace through the trial, by the Lord's grace.

## *Jesus Works Miracles for Parents*

The words of an Old Testament prophet can bring great comfort to parents who have suffered through estrangement with their adult kids. This old covenant promise (fulfilled as part of Jesus' ministry) is that "hearts of the fathers" will be turned to their children and the "hearts of the children to their fathers" (Mal. 4:6). The work of reconciliation is the work of our loving Savior. He's the only one who can turn our hearts toward our heavenly Father. He's the one who is able to turn the hearts of our kids to us and us to them.

During a trying time we were having with our adult children, a friend reminded me that several of Jesus' miracles were performed for children in answer to the pleas of their parents.[3] While it is true that Jesus' healings are signs that demonstrate his infinite power over the effects of sin and symbolize his work of delivering his people from its power, these miracles also assure us that he hears the cries of parents in anguish over their children.

Our heavenly Father has tasted the very anguish we feel when we're separated from our children because of sin— theirs or ours. He was separated from his beloved Son too, but not because he or his Son sinned. He was separated from his Son because of our sin. If he would so lovingly deny himself the joys of his Son for our sake, we can rest securely, knowing that he will always have compassion on those who turn to him in their need. He still has power to work miracles in the lives of our children, no matter how old they are. So cry out to him in prayer. He still hears. He completely understands. He has walked through every dark trial you're facing now. He has felt the separation that sin brings. Do you feel forsaken? Jesus cried out, "My God, my God, why have you forsaken me?" He knows about the emptiness that fills your heart and the hopelessness you feel. Let us encourage you again; take your heartache to Jesus. Pray for yourself. Pray for your children. Ask for deliverance and then humbly end with, "Not my will, but thine be done." Perhaps the Lord will restore everything you feel you've lost. Or, perhaps he'll give you grace to persevere and learn what it means to walk in his sufferings. In any case, you can rest securely, knowing that he'll never stop being your Father either.

# Appendix A
# Resolving Conflict
# with In-Laws

1. **Be quick to overlook minor offenses and slights** (1 Peter 4:8). Your son and his wife may have spent both Thanksgiving and Christmas Day with her parents, while only spending Christmas Eve with your family. If you're wise, you won't make an issue of it. Instead you can demonstrate gratitude and humility by being thankful they wanted to be with you at all. Or, perhaps you overhear your son-in-law say something unkind about your church. As Spurgeon said, "Turn your deaf ear to what you judge to be his harsh criticism."[1]

2. **Be very careful with your speech.** Scripture teaches us that we should "let no corrupting talk come out of [our] mouths, but only such as is good for building up, as fits the occasion, that it may give grace to those who hear" (Eph. 4:29). Proverbs teaches us that, "When words are many, transgression is not lacking, but whoever restrains his lips is prudent" (Prov. 10:19). We would be wise to remember

that one verbal outburst can damage a relationship for years to come. We should think very carefully before choosing to speak. A good question to ask is always, "Will what I have to say build up? Or am I just wanting to vent?"

3. **Get the beam out of your own eye** (Matt. 7:3–5). Because of the deceptive nature of sin, it is very easy for us to be quite blind to our own sins and faults. If you sense that something is wrong in your relationships, why not take time to examine yourself? If you aren't sure why your children seem alienated from you, ask them if there is anything you have done to offend them and if there is anything you can change to make your relationship with them better. It is also extremely important that, rather than defending yourself against their accusations, you make every effort to understand their perspective. For example, if they complain that you have been pressuring them, try to understand exactly what it is you do that bothers them. Then, in humility and respect, you can seek their forgiveness for not being more respectful of their marriage and sensitive to their feelings.

4. **Don't hold a grudge but be willing to forgive.** As Ephesians 4:32 says, "Be kind to one another, tenderhearted, forgiving one another, as God in Christ forgave you." The gospel is the key to successful relationships among sinners. We who have been forgiven much can offer forgiveness to those who have wronged us. Because Jesus paid the ultimate price so that we might be forgiven an infinite debt, we are able to forgive those who hurt us. Also, because we are to forgive in the same manner as God has forgiven us, it means that we are to remember their

sin against them no more (Jer. 31:33). When we forgive, we are promising to treat the person as God has treated us, which means we treat them as if they hadn't sinned against us. This also implies that we don't bring it up to that person, to others, or even to ourselves in our own thoughts. Failure to quickly forgive is a contradiction of the gospel and gives the devil an opportunity to gain a foothold in our family. "Be angry and do not sin; do not let the sun go down on your anger, and give no opportunity to the devil" (Eph. 4:26–27).

5. **Strive to understand their perspective**. Following in the footsteps of your Savior, Paul commands us to "do nothing from rivalry or conceit, but in humility count others more significant than your-selves. Let each of you look not only to his own interests, but also to the interests of others" (Phil. 2:3–4). We are often so caught up in our own side of a conflict that we have little understanding of the other person's point of view. Often we assume that if they would just pay better attention to what we have to say, the problem would be solved. In the midst of an argument we may sometimes find our-selves using the time someone else is speaking to "reload" our own argument rather than listening to what they are saying. The Bible teaches that we are to consider the interests of others as more impor-tant than our own. This is a key to peacemaking. When Daniel and his friends were on the verge of being forced to eat unclean Babylonian food, he was able to come up with a mutually agreeable solution by understanding that the Babylonian commander feared the consequences he would suffer if Daniel

and his friends didn't get proper nutrition and were scrawny. Do you understand why your daughter-in-law is reluctant to be around you? Do you understand why your son feels like you are still trying to control him? Rather than standing on your own perceived self-righteousness, ask yourself what you can do to understand and address their concerns.

6. **When you must confront sin, do so gently and carefully**. Remember that "if anyone is caught in any transgression, you who are spiritual should restore him in a spirit of gentleness. Keep watch on yourself, lest you too be tempted" (Gal. 6:1). When you are convinced that you must speak out or confront your married child and his spouse, be sure that your admonition is based upon Scripture and not merely your personal preferences. Pray before you speak that God will bless your efforts toward restoration and that the hearts of your loved ones will be prepared. Carefully plan how you will seek to gently appeal to them (Prov. 16:21; 25:11). Jesus likens bringing correction to removing a splinter from someone's eye (Matt. 7:5), which means that it is very delicate work. Also, remember that you cannot change or control them. Your hope is in God's transforming grace.

7. **Realize that you cannot make peace on your own**. "If possible, so far as it depends on you, live peaceably with all" (Rom. 12:18). While we are told to do everything in our power to pursue peace, sometimes peace remains out of reach. Some in-law relationships remain estranged for many years. We have known parents who have been completely shut out of the lives of their grown kids. They send birthday and

anniversary cards to their children and grandchildren only to have them sent back unopened. While this is heartbreaking, we encourage parents who are in this situation to continue to pursue peace with the prayer that the God of peace will soften the hearts of their children and bring about reconciliation.

# Appendix B
# Role Reversal: Children Caring for Parents

EDWARD, AGE FIFTY, has always been a good son. He visits his parents at least once a week and phones them every day to make sure they are okay. He has spent many Saturdays doing projects around their house. Two years ago he took over management of his parents' finances because their bank accounts and investments were in total disarray. Now, because of their health problems, including his father's dementia, Edward believes that his parents can no longer live on their own. He wants them to move into his home, but his wife, Natasha, isn't sure. She feels that he already spends too much time with them and fears that they will totally dominate the household if they move in. Edward's sister Christie is also causing trouble. Even though she has lived a self-centered life and hasn't taken an interest in caring for their parents until now, suddenly Christie is demanding to be included in every major decision. She has made statements implying that Edward is taking advantage of his position managing their parents' finances—abusing his power and maybe even cooking the books in his own favor.

Edward is beside himself with frustration. He has consistently done "the right thing," while Christie has been living irresponsibly in her own little world. Edward feels like giving up, but he knows that he must care for his parents and is trying to understand exactly what that should look like.

## Honor Your Father and Your Mother

We have already seen that while adult children are free from parental control, they still are responsible to honor their parents (Ex. 20:12). Adult children honor their parents when they seek their counsel regarding crucial decisions. They also show love and respect by investing in the relationship through frequent visits and phone calls. Many young families honor their parents who live far away by using their limited resources and vacation days to travel back home. This can produce lifelong memories and stronger bonds with our children and our grandchildren. As adult children gain a more mature perspective of adulthood, they should have grown in appreciation for how hard their parents' job really was, which should result in much gratitude and thanksgiving.

## Honor Your Parents by Ensuring Their Needs Are Met

Although many of us look forward to enjoying having fewer responsibilities during our empty-nest years, this is usually the same time that our aging parents begin to need more of our help. Jesus himself taught that we have an obligation to honor our parents, which includes ensuring that their material needs are met. He strongly condemned the Pharisees for using service to God as an excuse to avoid this duty (Matt. 15:3–6). Jesus even fulfilled this part of the Law while dying on the cross by making provisions for his mother because he could no longer care for her in his humanity. He gently committed her into the care of his beloved friend, the apostle John, who took her into his home (John 19:26–27). The apostle Paul commands children and grandchildren to provide for the financial needs of their widowed mothers and grandmothers before turning to the church for help (1 Tim. 5:4). In fact, he condemns those who do not meet this basic family obligation as worse than infidels (1 Tim. 5:8).

Sadly, our post-Christian culture is rapidly turning away from biblical values. The responsibility of caring for the aged has been transferred from the family to the state. Most grown children simply assume that it is the government's job to provide for their elderly parents. In addition, many older folks are lonely, even if their physical needs are being met by an institution. Their children are too busy with their own families and careers to have much time for grandma and grandpa. They assume that because their parents' physical needs are being met, they don't need visitors.

As our society sinks further into self-absorption, the elderly will suffer. The generation that learned to abort unwanted babies who would get in the way of their lifestyle is beginning to deal with their unwanted old people.[1] The percentage of elderly folks in our population will greatly increase as the baby boomers reach retirement age. There will be fewer workers paying taxes to fund Social Security, Medicare, and other programs for the elderly. Rising medical costs may increase social and political pressure to get unwanted elderly people out of the way either through euthanasia or by withholding care.[2] Politicians are already talking about the need to ration healthcare while questioning whether it is worthwhile to waste limited resources on non-productive people who aren't going to live much longer anyway.

## *Christians Have an Opportunity to Be Lights in the World*

Just as the early Christians demonstrated their value for life and their love for fellow human beings by caring for unwanted babies who had been left to die,[3] we have an opportunity to show forth the light of Christ by how we care for our elderly family members. Many Christian families have taken a widowed grandmother or an invalid grandfather into their homes so that they can spend their last days surrounded and cared for by those who love them. Others, whose parents can still live somewhat independently, spend a great deal of time helping mom and dad with various household tasks. Such love emulates the sacrificial love of Jesus, who sacrificed time, comfort, privacy, and money out of love for others. Taking care of an elderly parent can be extremely stressful, especially when you have to deal with their physical and mental infirmities. But we can show such love because we have been so loved (1 John 4:19).

### *Accepting Limitations*

When an elderly or needy parent moves in with her children, she'll want to remember that her son, or son-in-law, is now the head of the house. Perhaps she has had to live on her own for many years, but now she'll have to live under the authority of someone else. No matter how she may love that person it will be hard for her to accept this change in relationship.

One of the greatest challenges for older people is to accept new limitations. It's very difficult for them to admit that they cannot live alone any longer and that they should no longer drive or manage their own finances. They're also put in a position where they must humbly consider the needs and concerns of their family members (Matt. 7:12) by accepting and not resisting the limitations being placed upon them. If they have to deal with the distressing signs of early dementia, they'll also become frustrated when they realize that they're unable to think as clearly as they used to. A point comes when they will need to trust their loved ones who are of sound mind to make hard decisions for them.

The way to deal with these losses is to accept that God is sovereign and has taken back some of what he has given (Job 1:21). The good news for the believer is that these hardships are only temporary. Our blessed hope is that one day our infirmities will be no more; our bodies will be raised in the likeness of his glorious body at his return (Phil. 3:20–21). This sweet promise alone is strong enough to carry believers through the valley of the shadow of death—even a slow death like dementia or Alzheimer's.

Sometimes children with elderly parents come to us for counsel on how to handle their parents' unwillingness to receive help or to accept limitations. The children are fearful for their parents' safety while living alone, and perhaps the safety of others (in the case of elderly parents who should no longer be driving a vehicle). Children in this situation also need to recognize their own limited power. They usually cannot force their parents to act wisely, and relationships may be damaged if they try. Unless the parent is a significant danger to himself or others, you may have to wait patiently and trust the Lord to take care of them.

Another potential complicating factor is conflicts among siblings. The child who lives near the parents or who takes them into her home may feel that she is bearing too great a load while the others sit back. Those who live farther away may suspect that the child who is more involved in the parents' lives is taking advantage of her position by acquiring parental assets and heirlooms. It is very important that siblings communicate openly about these subjects and do so according to biblical principles of assuming the best (1 Cor. 13:7), overlooking minor faults (1 Peter 4:8), and considering the interests of others above one's own (Phil. 2:3–4).

Faithful living in the midst of these ongoing challenges may seem beyond your reach. Trying to balance the responsibility of caring for aging parents with the rest of your responsibilities (spouse, kids that live in your home, and kids who have moved out) will surely be overwhelming. Let us recommend that you seek biblical counsel from your pastor or from a biblical counselor who can help you sort out your varied responsibilities and prioritize them. You'll also find some recommended resources in the "Resources for More Help" section at the end of the book.

# Appendix C
# The Best News Ever

## ELYSE FITZPATRICK

I DIDN'T BEGIN to understand the gospel until the summer before my twenty-first birthday. Although I had attended church from time to time in my childhood, I'll admit that it never really transformed me in any significant way. I was frequently taken to Sunday school where I heard stories about Jesus. I knew, without really understanding, the importance of Christmas and Easter. I remember looking at the beautiful cranberry red and cerulean blue of a stained glass window that depicted Jesus knocking on a garden door and having a vague sense that being religious was good. But I didn't have the foggiest notion about the gospel.

When adolescence came barging in, my strongest memories are those of despair and anger. I was consistently in trouble, and I hated everyone who pointed that out. There were nights when I prayed that I would be good, or more specifically, that I would get out of whatever trouble I was in and start fresh, only to be disappointed and angered by the failures of the following day.

After graduating from high school at seventeen, I got married, had a baby, and divorced all before the second decade of my life began. It was during the following months and years that I discovered the anesthetizing effects of drugs, alcohol, and illicit relationships. Although I would have been known as a girl who liked to party, I was utterly lost and joyless, and I was beginning to know it.

At one point I can remember telling a friend that I felt like I was fifty years old, which at that point in my life was the oldest I could imagine anyone being. I was exhausted and disgusted, so I decided to set about improving myself. I worked a full-time job, took a full load at a local junior college, and cared for my son. I changed my living arrangements and tried to start over. I didn't know that the Holy Spirit was working in my heart, calling me to the Son. I just knew that something had to change. Don't misunderstand, I was still living a shamefully wicked life, it's just that I felt like I was beginning to wake up to something different.

Then Julie entered my life. She was my next-door neighbor, and she was a Christian. She was kind to me, and we became fast friends. She had a quality of life about her that attracted me, and she was always talking to me about her Savior, Jesus. She let me know that she was praying for me and would frequently encourage me to "get saved." Although I'd had that Sunday school training, what she had to say was something completely different from what I'd ever remembered hearing. She told me I needed to be born again.

And so, on a warm night sometime in June of 1971, I knelt down in my tiny apartment and told the Lord that I wanted to be his. I didn't really understand much about the gospel then, but I did understand this: I knew I was desperate, and

I desperately believed that the Lord would help me. That prayer on that night changed everything about me. I remember it now, thirty-five years later, as if it were yesterday. I knew I needed to be saved, and I trusted that he could save me. The Bible tells of a man who came in contact with some of Jesus' followers and asked this same question: "What must I do to be saved?" The answer was simple: "Believe in the Lord Jesus, and you will be saved."

Very simply, what do you need to believe in order to be a Christian? You need to know that you need salvation, help, or deliverance. You must not try to reform yourself or decide that you're going to become a moral person so that God will be impressed. Because he is completely holy, meaning perfectly moral, you have to give up any idea that you can be good enough to meet his standard. This is the good bad news. It's bad news because it tells you that you're in an impossible situation that you cannot change. But it's also good news because it will free you from endless cycles of self-improvement that end in ultimate failure.

You also need to trust that what you're unable to do— live a perfectly holy life—he has done for you. This is the good, good news. This is the gospel. Basically the gospel is the story of how God looked down through the corridors of time and set his love on his people. At a specific point in time, he sent his Son into the world to become fully like us. This is the story you hear about at Christmas. This baby grew to be a man, and after thirty years of obscurity he began to show the people who he was. He did this by performing miracles, healing the sick, and raising the dead. He also demonstrated his deity by teaching people what God required of them, and continually foretold his coming death and resurrection. And he did one more thing; he claimed to be God.

Because of his claim to be God, the leading religious people, along with the political powers of the day, passed an unjust sentence of death upon him. Although he had never done anything wrong, he was beaten, mocked, and shamefully executed. He died. Even though it looked like he had failed, the truth is that this was God's plan from the very beginning.

His body was taken down from the cross and laid hastily in a rock tomb in a garden. After three days, some of his followers went to go properly care for his remains and discovered that he had risen from the dead. They actually spoke with him, touched him, and ate with him. This is the story that we celebrate at Easter. After another forty days, he was taken back up into heaven, still in his physical form, and his followers were told that he would return to earth in just the same way.

I told you that there were two things you needed to know and believe. The first is that you need more significant help than you or any other merely human person could ever supply. The second is that you believe that Jesus, the Christ, is the person who will supply that help and that if you come to him, he will not turn his back on you. You don't need to understand much more than that, and if you really believe these truths, your life will be transformed by his love.

Below I've written out some verses from the Bible for you. As you read them, you can talk to God just as though he were sitting right beside you (because his presence is everywhere!), and ask him for help to understand. Remember that his help isn't based on your ability to perfectly understand or anything that you can do. If you trust him, he has promised to help you and that's all you need to know for now.

For all have sinned and fall short of the glory of God. (Romans 3:23)

For the wages of sin is death, but the free gift of God is eternal life in Christ Jesus our Lord. (Romans 6:23)

For while we were still weak, at the right time Christ died for the ungodly. For one will scarcely die for a righteous person—though perhaps for a good person one would dare even to die—but God shows his love for us in that while we were still sinners, Christ died for us. (Romans 5:6–8)

For our sake he made him to be sin who knew no sin, so that in him we might become the righteousness of God. (2 Corinthians 5:21)

If you confess with your mouth that Jesus is Lord and believe in your heart that God raised him from the dead, you will be saved. For with the heart one believes and is justified, and with the mouth one confesses and is saved. For the Scripture says, "Everyone who believes in him will not be put to shame." . . . The same Lord is Lord of all, bestowing his riches on all who call on him. For "everyone who calls on the name of the Lord will be saved." (Romans 10:9–13)

And whoever comes to me I will never cast out. (John 6:37)

Therefore, if anyone is in Christ, he is a new creation. The old has passed away; behold, the new has come. (2 Corinthians 5:17)

Come to me, all who labor and are heavy laden, and I will give you rest. Take my yoke upon you, and learn from me, for I am gentle and lowly in heart, and you will find rest for your souls. (Matthew 11:28–30)

There is therefore now no condemnation for those who are in Christ Jesus. (Romans 8:1)

If you'd like to, you might pray a prayer something like this: "Dear God, I'll admit that I don't understand everything about this, but I do believe these two things: I need help, and you want to help me. I confess that I'm like Elyse and pretty much ignored you my whole life except when I was in trouble or just wanted to feel good about myself. I know that I haven't loved you or my neighbor, so it's true that I deserve to be punished and really do need help. But I also believe that you've brought me here, right now, to read this page because you are willing to help me and that, if I ask you for help, you won't send me away empty-handed. I'm beginning to understand how you punished your Son in my place and how I can have a relationship with you because of his sacrifice for me. Father, please guide me to a good church and help me understand your word. I give my life to you and ask you to make me yours. In Jesus' name, Amen."

Here are two more thoughts. In his kindness, Jesus established his church to encourage and help us understand and live out these two truths. If you know that you need help, and you think that Jesus is able to supply that help, or if you're still questioning but want to know more, please search out a good church in your neighborhood and begin to make relationships there. A good church is one that recognizes that we cannot save ourselves by our own goodness and that relies wholly on Jesus Christ (and no one else) for this salvation. You can call around and ask these questions or you could even go on the Internet and get a listing of churches in your area. Usually they will have something called a "statement of faith" on their website, where you can get information about them. Mormons and Jehovah's Witnesses are not Christians, and they do not believe in the gospel (though they might tell you that they do). Finding a good church is sometimes quite a process, so don't be discouraged if you don't succeed right away. Keep trying and believing that God will help you.

Second, another factor that will help you grow in this new life of faith is to begin to read what God has said about himself and about us in his Word, the Bible. In the New Testament (the last third or so of the Bible), there are four Gospels or narratives about the life of Jesus. I recommend that you start with the first one, Matthew, and then work your way through the other three. I also recommend that you purchase a good modern translation, like the English Standard Version, but you can get any version that you're comfortable with (though not a paraphrase) and begin reading more right away.

The last request that I have of you is that you contact me through my website, www.elysefitzpatrick.com, if you've decided you want to follow Jesus through this book. Thank you for taking time to read this little explanation of the most important news you'll ever hear. You can begin to read this book now and trust that the Lord will help you understand and become what he wants you to be: a person who has been so loved by him that it transforms both your identity and your life.

# Appendix D
# Sample Contracts with Your Young Adults

**Typical expectations**

1. You will spend a minimum of fifty productive hours each week (school, work, helping around the house, volunteering). Exodus 20:8–9; 2 Thessalonians 3:10–12; Proverbs 6:6,9–11.
2. We will have an agreed-upon goal for this phase of your life while living at home (i.e., education, savings, etc.). Proverbs 21:5.
3. You will treat parents and other family members with respect. Exodus 20:12; Proverbs 30:17; Matthew 7:12.
4. You will show us the courtesy of letting us know where you are and when we can expect you to be home (including whether you will be with us at mealtimes). If you are coming in late, you will make every effort not to disturb those who are trying to sleep. Philippians 2:3–4.

5. You will help to keep our home neat and clean, especially public areas, but also your room, and will pitch in with family chores. Romans 15:2–3; Proverbs 10:5.
6. You will not engage in any illegal (e.g., drugs) or immoral (e.g., fornication, drunkenness, or viewing pornography) activity, whether inside or outside our home. 1 Thessalonians 5:7; Hebrews 13:4; Proverbs 20:1; 23:29–35; Romans 13:14.
7. You will be financially responsible (which may include paying your fair share of family expenses and/or rent). Proverbs 22:7.
8. Trust is most important. You must be honest with us. If you lie to us you are treating us as an enemy. Enemies can't live together. Ephesians 4:25.

### For a child who has persistently been in trouble

1. You will be subject to random drug and alcohol testing/screening any time we ask.
2. You will keep a written record of your productive hours to be turned in every Saturday evening.
3. You will make the agreed payments on your debt and will keep records of your income and expenditures.

### Consequences for failure to comply (Galatians 6:7)

1. Extra work around the house.
2. Financial fines: e.g., $10 for leaving items in the living area; $10 for a messy room; $15 for every hour under fifty productive hours per week.
3. Restitution: e.g., repaying parents for college or vocational classes not passed.
4. Taking away cell phone, computer, computer/Internet privileges, car, etc.

5. If you choose not to follow our rules and to accept the consequences for breaking the rules, you are effectively choosing to no longer live at home.

### What your child should be able to expect from you

1. We will make our expectations clear.
2. We will not nag, scold, or admonish in sinful anger. Matthew 5:21–22; Proverbs 25:28; James 1:19.
3. When dealing with conflict we will apply biblical peace-making principles.
4. We will not micromanage your life, but will show respect to you as a fellow adult.
5. We will listen. Proverbs 20:5; James 1:19.
6. We will admit when we are wrong. Matthew 5:23–24.
7. We will seek to assume the best. 1 Corinthians 13:7.
8. We will seek to make our home a place of joy and fun.

# Notes

**Introduction**

1. Lev Grossman, "Grow Up? Not So Fast," *Time*, January 16, 2005, http://www.time.com/time/magazine/article/0,9171,1018089,00. html.

2. *Money* magazine did a series of articles about financial relationships between parents and their adult kids.

3. The Barna Group, "Most Twentysomethings Put Christianity on the Shelf Following Spiritually Active Teen Years," Barna Group, http://www.barna.org/barna-update/article/16-teensnext-gen /147-most-twentysomethings-put-christianity-on-the-shelf-following-spiritually-active-teen-years.

4. Reb Bradley, "Solving the Crisis in Homeschooling," *Family Ministries*, http://www.familyministries.com/HS_Crisis.htm.

**Chapter One: Is It That Time *Already?***

1. Reb Bradley, "The Four Seasons of Child Training," *Family Ministries*, http://www.familyministries.com/4_Seasons_of_CT.htm.

2. Tedd Tripp, *Shepherding a Child's Heart* (Wallowopen, NJ: Shepherd Press, 1995), 236.

3. On page 201 of *Shepherding a Child's Heart* by Tedd Tripp, there is a chart that shows how the parenting process should work as a child approaches maturity. When a child is very young the parental focus is on control. As our children get older, our role becomes more about influence, and by the time they are adults our authority is gone.

4. Ken Sande, "First Visit? Please Read This," *Peacemaker Ministries,* http://www.peacemaker.net/site/c.aqKFLTOBIpH/b.937085 /k.A1EB/First_Visit_Please_Read_This.htm

5. When I told one of my adult sons the title for this book (*You Never Stop Being a Parent*) he suggested, somewhat in jest, that we just leave off the first two words.

6. John Piper, "A Church-Based Hope for 'Adultolescents,'" *Desiring God,* November 13, 2007, http://www.desiringgod.org /ResourceLibrary/TasteAndSee/ByDate/2007/2487_A_Church Based_Hope_for_Adultolescents/.

7. Almost everyone who teaches that Ephesians 6:1 still applies to grown children will admit that once a child is married the relationship with his parents changes (Gen. 2:24). Most will also agree that parental authority is limited and subject to God's authority: "We must obey God rather than men" (Acts 5:29, NASB).

## Chapter Two: Before You Walk Out That Door . . .

1. See *Opening Up Proverbs* by Jim Newheiser for more on getting the most out of Proverbs.

2. Lev Grossman, "Grow Up? Not So Fast," *Time,* January 16, 2005, http://www.time.com/time/magazine/article/0,9171,1018089,00. html.

3. Kate Antonovics, "Marriage Prospects: Richer, Not Poorer," *Kiplinger,* February 2005, http://www.kiplinger.com/magazine /archives/2005/02/interview.html.

4. "In the last five years I have heard countless reports of highly sheltered homeschool children who grew up and abandoned their parents' values. Some of these children were never allowed out of their parents' sight and were not permitted to be in any kind of group setting, even with other 'like-minded' kids, yet they still managed to develop an appetite for the world's pleasures. . . . Children . . . then come to view Christianity as mostly about 'avoiding bad stuff.' When protection from the world becomes *the defining characteristic of Christianity,* we shouldn't be surprised if our kids grow up and forsake the lifeless 'religion of avoidance' they learned from us. . . . After watching multitudes

of highly sheltered children grow up and chase after the very things from which their parents sought to keep them, and seeing less-sheltered children grow up and walk strong, I am more selective about which hill I want to die on. I now pick my battles more carefully. I have concluded that fruitful parenting is more about what we put into our children than what we protect them from." Reb Bradley, "Solving the Crisis in Homeschooling," *Family Ministries*, http://www.familyministries.com/HS_Crisis.htm.

### Chapter Three: You Say Good-Bye, but He Says Hello

1. John Piper, "A Church-Based Hope for 'Adultolescents,'" *Desiring God*, November 13, 2007, http://www.desiringgod.org /ResourceLibrary/TasteAndSee/ByDate/2007/2487_A_Church Based_Hope_for_Adultolescents/.

2. Marilyn Harris, "What Do You Owe Your Kids?" *Money*, March 2008, 103.

3. "An estimated 65 percent of college graduates have moved back in with their parents, according to the U.S. Census Bureau." Karina Bland, "For many grads, first big move is back home," The Arizona Republic, May 4, 2008, http://www.azcentral.com/news /articles/2008/05/04/20080504stayingput0504.html.

4. Marilyn Elias, "Kids and parents agree: 18- to 25-year-olds aren't adults," *USAToday*, December 12, 2007, http://www.usatoday.com/ news/health/2007-12-12-emerging-adults_N.htm.

5. Dan Kadlec, "Protecting Your Big Kid—and You," *Money*, September 2009, 34; Harris, "What Do You Owe Your Kids?"

6. Piper, "A Church Based Hope for 'Adultolescents'"; Albert Mohler, "The Generation That Won't Grow Up," *Albert Mohler*, January 24, 2005, http://www.albertmohler.com/commentary_read. php?cdate=2005-01-24; Alex and Brett Harris, "Addicted to Adolescence," *Boundless*, February 16, 2006, http://www.boundless .org/2005/articles/a0001217.cfm.

7. When our youngest son moved home after completing college he brought us closer together as a family by getting us to turn off the TV at night and play board games instead.

8. The acquisition of a marketable skill goes a long way in preparing our kids to take care of their own families one day (See Proverbs 22:29).

9. It is estimated that over three million disabled children are cared for by family members. University of Maine Cooperative Extension Aging Initiative Office, " Supporting Family Caregivers Conference," University of Maine Cooperative Extension, http://www.umext .maine.edu/AgingInitiatives/SupportingFamilyCaregivers Conference.htm.

10. See appendix B for more on taking care of needy parents.

11. David Brooks, "Navigating the Odyssey Years," *New York Times*, October 9, 2007, http://www.nytimes.com/2007/10/09/ opinion/09brooks.html.

12. Lev Grossman, "They Just Won't Grow Up," *Time,* January 16, 2005, http://www.time.com/time/covers/1101050124/.

13. *Time* magazine points out that only half of Americans in their mid-twenties earn enough to support a family. Ibid.

14. Ibid.

15. Ibid.

16. The median age for marriage is now up to twenty-six for women and twenty-eight for men. Information Please® Database, "Median Age at First Marriage, 1890–2007," *Pearson Education, Inc.*, http://www.infoplease.com/ipa/A0005061.html.

17. Albert Mohler, "The Generation That Won't Grow Up." *Albert Mohler,* January 24, 2005, http://www.albertmohler.com /commentary_read.php?cdate=2005-01-24.

18. Grossman, "They Just Won't Grow Up."

**Chapter Four: Saying Hello to Pleasing God**

1. Mick, a widower, has found it hard to finish raising his two children who were in high school when his wife passed away. Now that they are in their twenties, he is having an even more difficult time. His daughter Tina, twenty-six, had a child out of wedlock and has returned home, along with her two-year-old son Wesley, since breaking up with the boy's father. Tina does not work because she wants to be a full-time mom. Now she has a new boyfriend with whom she

goes out most evenings, often leaving Wesley with Grandad. Mick's son Sal, twenty-four, has never left home. He wants to start a surfing school but hasn't made much progress. Sal pays for his expenses with a credit card Mick lets him use. When Mick threatens to cut Sal and Tina off financially or kick them out of the house, they tell him that they are traumatized by the death of their mother and that he knows that she would never want him to break up the family this way. The latest complication is that Mick has met Silvia, a lovely, godly single woman who is a few years younger than he is. Their relationship was progressing wonderfully until Silvia saw the situation in Mick's home. She told Mick, "I will not even consider marrying you until you get those kids out of the house!"

**Chapter Five: You're Welcome to Stay, But . . .**

1. Troubles multiply when married adult children live with their parents. Genesis 2:24 says, "For this reason [marriage] a man shall leave his father and mother" (NASB). Ideally a young couple won't get married until they are able to live independently of their parents, both financially and emotionally. The idea of living with mom and dad can sometimes be appealing from the standpoint of saving money, but our observation has been that in virtually every case, even those who optimistically asserted that their family would be the exception to the rule, major tensions have erupted. Just as it is hard for a sapling to grow under the shadow of a full-grown tree, it is very hard for a young couple to fully develop in their marital roles with mom and dad around all of the time. When grandchildren are involved problems multiply because grandparents and parents often disagree over how the kids are disciplined. We realize that there may be exceptional circumstances due to a financial or medical emergency where a couple may be forced to temporarily move in with mom and dad. But even in these cases, we strongly encourage them to move out as soon as possible.

2. We lived for several years in a Middle Eastern country where the traffic laws were disregarded and virtually unenforced. It was scary!

3. Another couple, disappointed at their son's poor grades during his first year in college, informed him that he would have to pay for his own classes in advance and that they would reimburse his expenses for each course that he passed with at least a B grade.

## Chapter Six: Thanks, I'd Like to Stay, If . . .

1. A young adult writes that the worst things parents can do is "treat their adult kids like they are still children or compare their kids' success with their own. I could always tell when my parents were being loving by instructing me and correcting me versus when they were just mad and putting me down."

2. A young man writes, "The greatest challenge I have faced is dealing with my own expectations of 'success' compared with what my parents have accomplished and expect of me (or at least what I think they expect). I often worry if I will ever be as successful as my parents, and what they would think of me if I am not able to give to my children what they provided for me." One young woman writes, "The most challenging thing [about the transition to adulthood] for me has been trying to establish my role as wife and mother in the sight of my parents, my mom especially. . . . I felt as though she didn't see my husband and me as competent parents."

## Chapter Seven: Should Your Home Become a Halfway House?

1. Elyse Fitzpatrick and Jim Newheiser, *When Good Kids Make Bad Choices* (Eugene, OR: Harvest House Publishers, 2005).

2. The Lord himself knows what it is like to have wayward children as he bemoans Israel's rebellion: "Listen, O heavens, and hear, O earth; for the Lord speaks, sons I have reared and brought up, but they have revolted against Me" (Isa. 1:2, NASB; also see Jer. 2:30).

3. "I was overly-confident in my approach to parenting. I was convinced that my children would grow up godly, and that they would avoid significant struggles with sin because of my parenting. I was absolutely certain that since I was training them 'in the way they should go', and I was doing most everything I had written in my book, I would be a success as a parent. However, I had yet to discover it wasn't all about ME and MY success. In fact, I had yet to

learn that the parent who thinks it's all about THEIR success is often contributing to their children's struggles. . . .

I once believed and taught that a parent could follow the right biblical steps and be assured of raising children who remained faithful to God from childhood into their adult years. In fact, as a parent of young children I judged as a failure any parent whose young adult children were prodigal. However, as my own children aged and I discovered that they were self-determining individuals with their own walks with Christ, I came to the alarming realization that I had a lot of control over their outside, but not their inside. They were like **all** people who were faced with the choice of whether or not they were going to listen to Christ and follow him." Reb Bradley, "Solving the Crisis in Homeschooling," *Family Ministries*, http://www.familyministries.com/HS_Crisis.htm.

4. Abraham Piper, "12 Ways to Love Your Wayward Child," *Desiring God*, May 9, 2007, http://www.desiringgod.org/ResourceLibrary /TasteAndSee/ByDate/2007/2168_12_Ways_to_Love_Your _Wayward_Child/.

5. Albert Einstein, Quotation #26032, *The Quotations Page*, http://www.quotationspage.com/quote/26032.html.

6. One of the most complicated situations a parent will face is when the waywardness of their adult child negatively affects others, such as a wife and children. One couple, whose son was serving a long prison sentence for armed robbery, took his wife and children into their home.

7. One young man writes, "Threats may be appropriate! I am the recipient of a fatherly threat, and it was one of the most influential conversations I have ever had. Got my hormone-driven body under control and rational again. A real blessing, though he could have done it even sooner!"

8. When trust has been lost it must be earned back. Sean, who had been arrested twice for possession of illegal drugs, was offended by his parents' requirement that he take periodic drug screening tests as a condition for living at home. "You don't trust me!" he complained. "You're right!" replied his mother, Cheryl. "Taking the drug test gives you the opportunity to regain our

trust." Second Corinthians 7:10–11 contrasts a worldly sorrow with godly sorrow. Many people are sorry when they are caught doing something wrong because of the consequences they must face. Those who are truly repentant hate what they have done because it was a sin against God, they are concerned about the people they have hurt, and they are willing to do whatever it takes to avoid repeating their past sins. They welcome accountability because they don't trust themselves. They want to change and they want to make things right.

9. A. Piper, "12 Ways to Love Your Wayward Child."

## Chapter Eight: Wisely Navigating the Money Maze

1. U.S. Department of the Treasury, "The Debt to the Penny and Who Holds It," *Treasury Direct*, http://www.treasurydirect.gov/NP /NPGateway.

2. Ben Woolsey and Matt Schulz, "Credit Card Statistics, Industry Facts, Debt Statistics," *CreditCards*, January 15, 2010, http:// www.creditcards.com/credit-card-news/credit-card-industry-facts-personal-debt-statistics-1276.php.

3. Chad Hills, "FAQ: Gambling in the U.S." *CitizenLink*, April 30, 2008, http://www.citizenlink.org/FOSI/gambling/cog/A000007294 .cfm.

4. Marilyn Harris, "What Do You Owe Your Kids?" *Money*, March 2008, 103.

5. It is almost impossible for a young adult to go to college without financial help from her parents, especially if the parents have income or assets, because financial aid allotment is based on what a college thinks the family can afford. A top-flight college may cost tens of thousands of dollars a year, which makes it almost impossible for a student to work to put herself through school.

6. One young recipient of mercy writes, "By the time we reach adulthood, we are responsible for our own actions and cannot expect our parents to come to our rescue because we messed up. That being said, I found myself in a less than desirable financial state and needed help. My mother found out while sorting through some car insurance plans for me. I had a plan to pay it off by the end of the

summer, but it would have taken over a month. My mother counseled me about my lifestyle, showing me how I was living above my means, especially because I had no income this past school year. Since I did not expect them to help me, I was deeply impacted by having to face a real problem that had serious consequences. If I had expected them to pay for it and they had, then I would have thought that I just had gotten a free ride. I don't think that a parent bailing a child out when they expect it is beneficial, but if they don't feel entitled to the help, it can be a beautiful picture of undeserved grace and a valuable learning experience."

7. Joseph Belcher, *The Religious Denominations in the United States* (Indianapolis: Spicer & Roll, 1857), 183.

## Chapter Nine: Marriage: Our Dreams, Their Dreams

1. The comedian Andy Griffith suggests, "The moral of it is; if you got a boy that courts a girl that you don't like, or the other way around, if you don't want the expense of a double funeral on ya, the best thing to do is to let 'em have a cheap weddin'." Andy Griffith, "Romeo and Juliet—Explained . . ." *Epicure,* http://www.epicure .demon.co.uk/romeoandjuliet.html.

2. One parent wisely points out that we should also have concern for the people our children will marry. We know our own kids' sins and weaknesses best of all.

3. "They said, 'Let us call the young woman and ask her.' And they called Rebekah and said to her, 'Will you go with this man?' She said, 'I will go'" (Gen. 24:57–58).

4. "If anyone thinks that he is not behaving properly toward his betrothed, if his passions are strong, and it has to be, let him do as he wishes: let them marry—it is no sin. But whoever is firmly established in his heart, being under no necessity but having his desire under control, and has determined this in his heart, to keep her as his betrothed, he will do well. So then he who marries his betrothed does well, and he who refrains from marriage will do even better" (1 Cor. 7:36–38).

5. The author explains that as God has made all things he has the right to do with what belongs to him as he pleases (Rom. 9:21).

What the author misses, however, is that it is God, not earthly fathers, who ultimately creates and owns daughters. God expresses his will through his Word, which many earthly fathers fail to follow.

6. Sarah Faith Schlissel, "Daddy's Girl: Courtship and a Father's Rights," *BibleTopics*, http://www.bibletopics.com/BIBLESTUDY/92b.htm.

7. Bill Gothard, "What Is Courtship?" *Bill Gothard*, http://billgothard.com/bill/teaching/courtship/.

8. It is interestingly inconsistent that Gothard says that parents do not have the authority to force their children to marry a particular person or even to marry at all. If parental authority is absolute such that parents can sinfully and selfishly forbid one marriage, why can't they sinfully command another?

9. Church leaders may determine that the parents used their authority unreasonably in the same way that church leaders may receive a person into membership who had been under discipline in another church after concluding that the discipline was exercised in an unbiblical way.

10. One daughter reports, "My parents actually tried to ruin our wedding . . . by contacting relatives far and wide to inform them that they were boycotting the wedding and that if the relatives decided to attend it, my parents would cut them off from the family."

11. Some have gone so far as to cut their child's image out of family group photographs.

12. Some would argue for shunning our disobedient children using 1 Corinthians 5:11 where Paul teaches that we are not to even eat with immoral people. The context is church discipline, which applies only to professing Christians. If your child does not profess to be a believer, then this text clearly has no application to the situation. If your sinful child claims to be a believer, our understanding is that you cannot engage in Christian fellowship with him or her (i.e., a mutual discussion of spiritual things), but that does not preclude family relationships. (For example, we don't think that a woman whose husband has been disciplined for being a swindler would be forbidden from eating with or speaking to her husband.)

13. It is profound that Joseph treats his brothers who had sold him into slavery as forgiven, embracing and helping them in Genesis 45, even though there is no record of their explicitly seeking forgiveness until many years later in Genesis 50.

14. When my children were still small, the adult son of a friend of mine eloped with his girlfriend in Las Vegas. I saw how this affected my friend and his wife, especially since her parents were included and he and his wife were excluded. Several days after the wedding my friend and his wife hosted a reception for his son and new daughter-in-law. My first reaction was, "Why would you do this for your son after he has so hurt and shamed you?" But then I realized that my friend did exactly the right thing, showing grace to his son and building bridges toward a relationship that God richly blessed in the following years.

15. One daughter tells of her tragic experience with her parents, "Continuing to deny fellowship with an adult child who has made a decision you disagreed with unless he apologizes for that decision is a poor way to influence one's children. I think my parents believed that to prevent their other children from falling away, as they perceived I had, they needed to make an example out of me. Unfortunately, that has had the exact opposite effect on my brothers and sisters. Rather than coming to my parents when differences arise, they do everything they possibly can to conceal what is going on in their life from my parents. . . . Our family is now full of walled-off relationships."

16. Mark Regnerus, "The Case for Early Marriage," *Christianity Today*, August 2009, http://www.christianitytoday.com/ct/2009/august/16.22.html.

17. Albert Mohler, "The Case for (Early) Marriage," *Crosswalk*, August 3, 2009, http://www.godrev.com/disprss/?/Crosswalk/focus/2536535/The-Case-for-Early-Marriage.html.

18. "While celebrating the call to life long singleness, the church [should] not encourage those who don't have the call to wait till late in their twenties or thirties to marry, even if it means marrying while in school." John Piper, "A Church-Based Hope for 'Adultolescents,'" *Desiring God*, November 13, 2007,

http://www.desiringgod.org/ResourceLibrary/TasteAndSee
/ByDate/2007/2487_A_ChurchBased_Hope_for_Adultolescents/.

## Chapter Ten: Your New Math: Adding by Subtracting

1. Wayne Mack, "In-laws: Married with Parents" (Phillipsburg, NJ: P&R Publishing, 2009).

2. Do not speak ill to your child (or to anyone else) about his or her spouse. It is wrong, and it will probably come back to bite you. One daughter reports, "There have been times with my mother-in-law when . . . she talks about her other daughters-in-law, critiques how they are, and brings up the mistakes they have made. I wonder if she does the same about me to them."

3. Sadly, we have seen cases in which an ultra-controlling (and borderline abusive) son-in-law keeps a daughter from her parents because he sees them as a threat to his authority and control. In other cases, it is the insecure daughter-in-law who shuts out her husband's parents from their marriage. We've also seen some parents tempted to jealousy when they sense that their child and his spouse are closer to the other in-laws, or if the other in–laws are able to be more generous through financial help and gifts.

Sometimes parents grieve when they see their child suffering in a very hard marriage. You must remember that your child chose his spouse, and it is his responsibility to live with the consequences of that decision. If they have a fight or disagreement, keep your distance and don't automatically take your child's side. If she seeks your counsel, focus upon her duty before God to love her husband, even if he is hard to love (I Peter 3:1) and to do all that is within her power to keep her marriage together. A mom writes, "Don't let your daughter unload on you and don't take sides with her. Listen, nod your head, maybe ask a question or two, and then send her home to her husband to work it out. Remind her of her need to submit lovingly to his leadership and pray like crazy if it seems hard. Jesus said, 'What God has joined together let no man separate.' "

4. Ken Sande, *The Peacemaker: A Biblical Guide to Resolving Conflict* (Grand Rapids: Baker, 2004).

5. Old West cowboys, not the Dallas football Cowboys!

6. See also Deuteronomy 6:2 and Exodus 10:2.

7. Robert Bernstein, "Nearly Half of Preschoolers Receive Child Care from Relatives," *U.S. Census Bureau News*, February 28, 2008, http://www.census.gov/Press-Release/www/releases/archives/children/011574.html.

8. Mike Bergman, "Single-Parent Households Showed Little Variation Since 1994, Census Bureau Reports," *U.S. Census Bureau News*, March 27, 2007, http://www.census.gov/Press-Release/www/releases/archives/families_households/009842.html.

## Conclusion: It Still Hurts Because You Never Stop Being a Parent

1. John Piper, "The Sorrows of Fathers and Sons," *Desiring God*, July 15, 2009, http://www.desiringgod.org/Blog/1912_the_sorrows_of_fathers_and_sons/.

2. John Calvin, *Sermons on 2 Samuel*, trans. Douglas F. Kelly (Edinburgh: Banner of Truth, 1992), 280.

3. The raising of Jairus' daughter (Mark 5:22–43); the healing of the nobleman's son (John 4:46–54); the boy possessed by a demon (Matt. 17:14–21); the Syrophoenician woman's daughter (Matt. 15:22–28); the raising of the son of the widow of Nain (Luke 7:11–17).

## Appendix A: Resolving Conflict with In-Laws

1. Charles H. Spurgeon, "The Blind Eye and the Deaf Ear," *Lectures to My Students* (New York: Robert Carter & Brothers, 1889), 250.

## Appendix B: Role Reversal: Children Caring for Parents

1. "Why is it that we heap scorn on 'deadbeat' parents who fail to take care of underage children, but excuse adult children who don't take care of their feeble parents? Perhaps it is because caring for children—no matter how many diapers and scrapes must be tended to—is a joyful experience, while aging involves untold sadness and indignity. Maybe it has something to do with our unwillingness to confront death. . . . Watching parents become chronically ill or senile is unbearably painful

for their adult children. The secular world . . . seeks to move death out of view—into thick-walled hospitals and under the care of professional doctors, nurses, and funeral directors. . . . The commandment to honor and love our elders never expires, giving us an opportunity to love others as Christ has loved us." Mollie Ziegler Hemingway, " 'Honor Thy Father' for Grownups," *Christianity Today*, July 1, 2009, http://www.christianitytoday.com/ct/2009/july/12.52.html.

2. Perhaps there will be protests with people carrying signs, "Every grandparent a wanted grandparent."

3. Elizabeth Lev, "The Return of Infanticide, Infant Exposure," Catholic Online, September 5, 2008, http://www.catholic.org/politics/story.php?id=29115.

# Resources for More Help

## Marriage

Harvey, Dave. *When Sinners Say I Do: Discovering the Power of the Gospel for Marriage.* Wapwallopen, PA: Shepherd Press, 2007.

Mack, Wayne. *A Homework Manual for Biblical Living: Family and Marital Problems.* Phillipsburg, NJ: P&R Publishing, 1980.

Mack, Wayne. *Strengthening Your Marriage.* Phillipsburg, NJ: P&R Publishing, 1999.

Mack, Wayne. *Sweethearts for a Lifetime: Making the Most of Your Marriage.* Phillipsburg, NJ: P&R Publishing, 2006.

Piper, John. *This Momentary Marriage: A Parable of Permanence.* Wheaton, IL: Crossway, 2009.

Ricucci, Gary. *Love That Lasts: When Marriage Meets Grace.* Wheaton, IL: Crossway, 2007.

## The Husband's Role

Priolo, Lou. *The Complete Husband: A Practical Guide to Biblical Husbanding.* Amityville, NY: Calvary Press, 2005.

Scott, Stuart. *The Exemplary Husband: A Biblical Perspective.* Bemidji, MN: Focus Publishing, 2002.

## The Wife's Role

Fitzpatrick, Elyse. *Helper by Design: God's Perfect Plan for Women in Marriage.* Chicago, IL: Moody Publishers, 2003.

Peace, Martha. *The Excellent Wife: A Biblical Perspective.* Bemidji, MN: Focus Publishing, 1999.

## Parenting

Fitzpatrick, Elyse, Jim Newheiser, and Laura Hendrickson. *When Good Kids Make Bad Choices: Hope and Help for Hurting Parents.* Eugene, OR: Harvest House Publishers, 2005.

Peace, Martha, and Stuart Scott. *The Faithful Parent: A Biblical Guide to Raising a Family.* Phillipsburg, NJ: P&R Publishing, 2010.

Ray, Bruce. *Withhold Not Correction.* Phillipsburg, NJ: P&R Publishing, 1978.

Tripp, Tedd. *Shepherding a Child's Heart.* Wapwallopen, PA: Shepherd Press, 1995.

Tripp, Paul. *Age of Opportunity: A Biblical Guide to Parenting Teens.* Phillipsburg, NJ: P&R Publishing, 2001.

## Caring for Aging Parents

Fitzpatrick, Elyse. *The Afternoon of Life: Finding Purpose and Joy in Midlife.* Phillipsburg, NJ: P&R Publishing, 2004.

**Jim Newheiser** is a pastor of Grace Bible Church in Escondido, California, and is the director of the Institute for Biblical Counseling and Discipleship. He holds a doctor of ministry and a master's degree from Westminster Seminary California, and he speaks at conferences and trains leaders both in the US and internationally. He is the author of *Opening Up Proverbs* and a co-author of *When Good Kids Make Bad Choices*. Newheiser is a fellow of the National Association of Nouthetic Counselors and a board member of the Fellowship of Independent Reformed Evangelicals. He and his wife Caroline have three adult sons.

**Elyse Fitzpatrick** holds a master's degree in biblical counseling from Trinity Theological Seminary and has been counseling women since 1989. She presently counsels for her church at the Institute for Biblical Counseling and Discipleship. She is a frequent retreat and conference speaker. Fitzpatrick co-authored *Women Helping Women*, a 1998 Gold Medallion finalist; she's the author of over a dozen books including *Idols of the Heart* and *Counsel from the Cross*. This is the second book that she has collaborated on with Jim Newheiser. She and her husband, Philip, have three adult children and six grandchildren.

# Also by Elyse Fitzpatrick

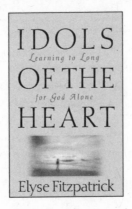

IDOLS
*Learning to Long*
OF THE
*for God Alone*
HEART

Elyse Fitzpatrick

Price: $13.99
To order, visit www.prpbooks.com
Or call 1(800) 631-0094

Many people desire to live godly lives but feel trapped in habitual sins. This book reveals that at the heart of every besetting sin lies idolatry.

"With great clarity and intriguing biblical illustrations, Fitzpatrick explains how idols in our hearts compete with our affections for God. . . . I highly recommend this book."

—MARTHA PEACE

"Fitzpatrick shows how Jesus Christ retakes our lives from these idols, setting up his reign over our attention, loyalty, and affections."

—DAVID POWLISON

# Also by Elyse Fitzpatrick

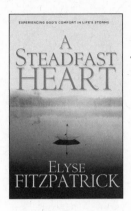

Price: $12.99
To order, visit www.prpbooks.com
Or call 1(800) 631-0094

Although never our personal choice, it is frequently God's plan that his children walk through storms and difficulties. Here readers will discover the secret of experiencing God's presence and comfort in trials and will grow in their appreciation of his purposes in their lives.

"If you are longing for a safe place in which to learn how to trust God in the unexplainable hurts in your life or the lives of loved ones, let Elyse help guide you."

—SHARON W. BETTERS

"With characteristic compassion that never compromises biblical principles, the author turns our gaze away from ourselves and onto Almighty God."

—LYDIA BROWNBACK

# More from P&R Publishing

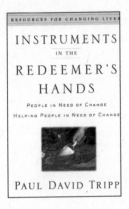

Price: $16.99
To order, visit www.prpbooks.com
Or call 1(800) 631-0094

Paul Tripp helps us discover where change is needed in our own lives and the lives of others. Following the example of Jesus, Tripp reveals how to get to know people, and how to lovingly speak truth to them.

"Helps us help others (and ourselves) by giving grace-centered hope that we can indeed change, and by showing us the biblical way to make change happen."

—Skip Ryan

"Tripp unites a loving heart with a mind trained to the Scriptures. This book is a great companion for pastors and counselors. It will guide anyone who wants to give real help to others, the saving help that is found in Christ's redeeming work."

—Richard D. Phillips

# More from P&R Publishing

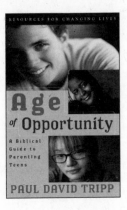

Price: $14.99
To order, visit www.prpbooks.com
Or call 1(800) 631-0094

Paul Tripp uncovers the heart issues affecting parents and their teenagers during the often chaotic adolescent years. With wit, wisdom, humility, and compassion, he shows parents how to seize the countless opportunities to deepen communication, learn, and grow with their teenagers.

"*Age of Opportunity* is a marvel. It brims with fresh, rich, honest truth. Tripp will get you looking in the mirror before you go looking at your teen. He'll get you seeking—and finding—your own Father's help."

—David Powlison

"A wealth of biblical wisdom and a treasure of practical steps for understanding and shepherding your teen's heart."

—Tedd Tripp

# More from P&R Publishing

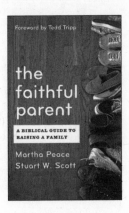

Price: $14.99
To order, visit www.prpbooks.com
Or call 1(800) 631-0094

Parents and children need help from the One who is perfect, who understands our need, and who can really help us. Martha Peace and Stuart Scott join forces to challenge you to become a faithful parent—one who perseveres and leaves the results to God.

"*The Faithful Parent* provides the comprehensive help that parents need. . . . The authors are seasoned Christians who are safe spiritual guides. . . . This will be a timeless resource for faithful parents."

—TEDD TRIPP

"I wholeheartedly recommend this book. . . . Thank you, Stuart and Martha, for providing a parenting book that is biblical, practical and specific."

—WAYNE A. MACK

# More from P&R Publishing

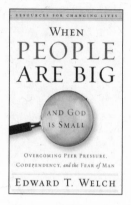

Price: $14.99
To order, visit www.prpbooks.com
Or call 1(800) 631-0094

"Need people less. Love people more. That's the author's challenge . . . He's talking about a tendency to hold other people in awe, to be controlled and mastered by them, to depend on them for what God alone can give. . . . [Welch] proposes an antidote: the fear of God."

—*Dallas Morning News*

"Biblical and practical. . . . Opens our eyes and directs us back to God and his Word to overcome the fear of man."

—*The Baptist Bulletin*

"Much needed in our own day. . . . Here is a volume that church libraries and book tables ought to have. Its theme is contemporary. Its answer is thoroughly biblical."

—*The Presbyterian Witness*